Pen

Will Write the

Way

MaryLou DeCarlo

MaryLou DeCarlo

ISBN 978-1-0980-1337-0 (paperback)
ISBN 978-1-0980-1338-7 (digital)

Christian Faith Publishing, Inc.
832 Park Avenue
Meadville, PA 16335
www.christianfaithpublishing.com

Scripture was taken from the New International Bible.
Cover design by Melaina Roberto.

Printed in the United States of America

To Jesus, Lover of my soul. "I will send you helpers," said the Lord, and so he did.

Contents

Acknowledgments

I am thankful to my Lord and Savior Jesus Christ who gave me a vision. His hand over my hand and the words "The pen will write the way."

I thank my children Kim, Dina, and Joe, their spouses Vin, Jeff, and Jen as well as my grandchildren Stephen, Matthew, Joseph, Jeffrey, Kristin, Mclaina, Danny, and Jake for their belief in me and their constant encouragement to walk my path.

I thank my dear cousin Mindy, whose relentless pursuit encouraged, inspired, and assisted me in collating my work and bringing it to completion.

I thank my dear cousin Anthony, who was diligent in keeping our working appointments, enabling this to be completed.

I thank my dear mentor Harry, who changed my life with the simple beautiful words "He is your best Lover, let him have his way."

I thank my dear friend and trainer Steve, who assisted in keeping me physically fit so I could continue my work for Jesus.

I thank my family Ben, Carolyn, Barbara, and Debbie who encouraged me.

I thank my Christian friends who prayed with me in song and worship to our beautiful Savior Jesus Christ.

Foreword

Marylou grew up in a Catholic home with her parents and siblings. She was sent to Catholic school for her early education and realized at a very early age that her peace was found in the house of God. Her desire at that time was to become a nun and longed to dress and worship as one.

As she grew up, her focus changed. She married, had three children, and spent her time with the activities of her family. The one thing that never changed was her love for God. After thirty years of marriage, her family dynamics changed, and a serious medical situation found Marylou searching for inner peace.

Although never thinking of herself as a good writer, she was influenced to begin journaling her thoughts to bring her closer to Jesus and that peace she wanted. In that journal, Marylou soon experienced wondrous things. She began to have dreams with conversations with Jesus. The change in her writing, wording, and focus changed as well.

I had the fortunate gift of her allowing me to read her journal. I cannot explain how reading this changed my life. Here was someone I knew as an ordinary being—not clergy, not a famous person—sharing a special gift with me and showing me how Jesus does come to you if you are willing to listen and learn.

I hope by sharing her words with you, you will be inspired as I have to walk the path that God has set for us and embrace his love and wisdom.

Mindy Apicella

First Encounters

(GOD'S UNDERSTANDING)

Lord, how do you see me?

The Lord answered

"My little one, I see you as a frightened child with the desire to obey and get close to me. There is no reason to be frightened. I am your Lord, and I am your Savior. I have chosen you in the convent where you first met me and we had our first encounter. Focus on that day of peace and know that I want to give you peace, wisdom, wealth, and good health all the days of your life. There is so much more I want to give you, but you block it with the thoughts of things that are not good for you. Keep your eyes on me, my child. I know what is best for you. Rebuke all that is not of me. I will show you the way. I

love you, little one. That is the name for you, little one. Go in peace today with love in your heart and a big smile on your face. I will show you the way. Let me lead you, little one. This is the day the Lord has made, let us rejoice and be glad. Enjoy my blessings."

Thank you, Jesus

My Dreams

(FAITH IN PRAYERS)

What an incredible evening I had last night at church. The Bible study began with Genesis, and it was very long. I was tired but interested. The leader of the group Dee paired people off to bless each other and speak what they felt God wanted to say to them. All I could think about was what I was going to say. I sat, quietly listening to them praying and speaking. Some spoke in tongues. The new people were paired to pray for one another. The leader chose to pray for me. I said to myself, "Okay, what do I say? I don't even know how to pray for these people." The leader began blessing me and told me that Jesus wanted to give me all my heart's desires. That he was going to make my dreams come true. I kept thinking, I did not have any great dreams or desires. What was she talking about? But as I sit here, my dreams are for the well-being of

15

my family. That each of my grandchildren is blessed with knowledge and a soft heart so they may prosper and become what God has intended them to be. I dream that they come to know and love Jesus and learn about his goodness. That they begin to receive his blessings and that they bless others. I pray they will live a peaceful life. I dream that my children stay healthy and that their marriages are blessed. That they feel the peace and beauty of God's love. I dream that they are able to give back to others in your name. I dream that my siblings, friends, and other family members come to know and love you. I dream that you are gentle in your teachings to all of them.

I dream that you fill my heart with love and peace so that I can help others and become all that you intend me to be. I dream of freedom to love and help this world become a better place. I dream for the wisdom to know what is right and wrong and to continue to know your love. I dream of a healthy body so I may fulfill all the work you have in store for me. I dream for the finances that will help me to accomplish all the work.

My blessings for the leader Dee of the group were that God gives her the wisdom and strength to do her work and that she has the health and wisdom to put her work in perspective so she may continue to do God's work. She will be pulled in many directions. May she have the strength and courage to say no to the things that are not important and yes to the important things. She said my prayer was right on and that I was good at praying. She then invited me to become part of the church. For the first time, I felt at home there.

She then walked off and got a tissue and dried her tears.

Thank you Jesus for a wonderful evening.

The Time Is Now, Said the Lord

(GOD'S TIMING)

Good morning, Father, the thunder roars, the rain falls, and yet there is still a feeling of peace in the air. It brings a smile to my face as I think of my childhood. "The Angels are bowling," my mom would say. Sometimes, I envision what it would be like in heaven. Oh, Father, there is such victory, love, and peace in following you. I feel sad for those who deny themselves this privilege of walking and accepting you as their Lord and Savior.

There it is again, a roar of thunder. The rain falls gently. The earth is soaking up your blessings of water to nurture it and bring back its color and beauty for your glory and those who have eyes to see it, ears to hear it, and not take it for granted, just as you bring us back from the captivity from our own hearts and minds.

Father, you woke me up this morning and spoke to me about the book you want me to complete for you. It will help your people come to know, trust, believe, and love you as I do. Father, what are you saying to me?

The Lord answered

"It is time child, it is time. It is time for you to move. It is time for you to recapture your health. It is time for you to do my work; it is time for you to write that book! It is time for you to grow up in me. Oh my child, you have struggled way to long. Oh my child, it pains me to see your struggle, as a Mom and Dad are pained to see their hurting children, I am pained to see your struggle. You are in control. You asked me yesterday, Father, when do we stop blaming the enemy and take control of our own minds? The time is now. The time is now little one for you to take control, take up your sword and fight the battle set before you. David was not afraid of Goliath, with a slingshot and a stone he slayed Goliath. Who then my child are you afraid of? Who then my child shall stand in the way of the daughter of the King of Kings, Lord of Lords, true God of true God's, the God most high? Yes little one, you are my child. You are mighty, you are strong, you are courageous, my will, will be done in your life, the time is now."

"I have sent you helpers, one to physically get your strength back, I have sent you helpers to mentally help your mind and prepare you. You will, you can, and you must do this for me. Yes child, I am a gentle God, yes child, I am a loving and merciful God, yes child, my grace is sufficient for you. All this is true, now capture it, claim it, and do it. I love you little one. I look forward to see your progress. I look forward to see the smile on your face as you help others to know who I am. I smile to see the unbelievers. I smile because you bring them to me and now they are believers. In your mind this is a great task. In your heart you know you can and will do this because your heart is for me. Your love for me shall now prevail, just as my love for you will always prevail. Go in peace today little one. Go in peace for it is time for you, little five foot child, to grow into the Goliath that has no fear, No, forget Goliath, the David who has slain Goliath. You will slay whatever it is that is holding you back. You will slay whatever it is trying to keep you from doing my work. I chose you because I knew your love for me. I chose you because I knew you would be obedient to me. I chose you because your faith would grow because you believe my words. I will take care of you and your family. Go in peace little one, go in peace today and *when you wake up, you will write. When you wake and begin to start the day you will begin with thankfulness in your heart and watch the blessings I have in store for you."*

Father, your grace is sufficient for me. Your will be done. Thank you, Lord and my Savior, for choosing me. I once said to myself that I am not Gideon, I am not David. I now know that I do not have to be; all I have to be is obedient to your voice.

*****

Thank you, my Father, I love you.
For I know the plans I have for you, declares the Lord, plans to prosper you and not to harm you, plans to give you hope and a future.

—Jeremiah 29:11

No weapon forged against you will prevail and you will refute every tongue that accuses you. This is the heritage of the servants of the Lord, and this is their vindication from me.

—Isaiah 54:17

Surely God is my salvation; I will trust and not be afraid. The Lord, the Lord himself, is my strength and defense; he has become my salvation.

—Isaiah 12:2

The Lord replied, "My presence will go with you, and I will give you rest."

—Exodus 33:14

David was greatly Distressed because the men were talking of stoning him, each one was bitter in spirit because of their sons and his daughters. But David found strength in the Lord his God.

—Samuel 30:6

What Direction Shall I Go?

(GUIDANCE)

Good morning, Father, in which direction do I go? Help me to be humble and steadfast to you and your word. I am yours, Father. Let your will be done in my life, not mine. Father, your grace is sufficient for me. Your kindness, greatness, and love are all that I need.

In which direction do I walk, Father?

The Lord answered

"Oh, my child, keep your eyes on me. You still seek approval from others. The only need for approval is from me. Mere men are of the flesh. I am the spirit that guides and loves you. Keep praying and asking for answers. They will come. As you have told others, lis-

ten to your heart. *That is my Holy Spirit directing your steps. Remember, if you miss an opportunity I have given you, I will somehow bring it back. Use opportunities as a platform for me, to spread my word and help those in need.*"

Show me how to hear you correctly.

The Lord answered

"*Oh, little one, remember what I said, if any of my children miss an opportunity I present, I will bring it back to them at a different time. Give them a chance.*"

"*Keep going, stay steadfast, and keep your eyes on me. Stay in love and peace. Always remember my love for you and all you love.*"

"*Branch out, little one. Time to take my love and word outside your home. Keep moving, my child. Always remember that I died and rose again for you. Now die unto yourself and surrender everything to me, for I am the truth, the way, and the life.*"

"*Stop worrying what others think. Do not slide back. Keep your eyes on me!*"

"*I love you, little one. You heard me so clearly the day the pastor said 'I'm going to let God speak to you.'*"

Be Obedient to God's Direction

(GUIDANCE)

It has been placed on my heart that I keep coming to you for direction and you keep giving me answers. But though I clearly hear your answers and write about them, I still do not act on them.

Like a child that asks for gifts from their parents, their requests are granted, and the child does not care for them properly and mistreats the beautiful gifts given to them. He takes them for granted. So it is with me. I repent for my sin of lack of respect and gratitude for the beautiful gift of guidance you provide me when I ask, "Father, please give me a word of guidance." I have taken your words and answers for granted and treated them lightly. Thank you for opening my eyes to see this as I come humbly before you with repentance for my carelessness with your teachings. It is no wonder I am stuck like the shadow of a man and child I saw in the doorway. I am standing, blocking my own path, blocking all that you have promised me. You have given me the key to unlock my heart from bondage and free myself to do your work. Let your will be done.

Father, what is the dream of a man with a gift and smiling at me? He is bringing me a blue-and-white gift with a razor and key on a green spiral cord. You have showed all this to me in several dreams. Father, what does this mean?

The Lord answered

"You know the answers, child. Fear not, I am with you. I will hold you with my victorious right hand. Yes, you asked about the razor. This does not necessarily mean cut things out. It means sharpen your mind, heart, and body. Sharpen your skills. Sharpen your sword. Be ready to cut down the enemy. Archangel Michael has a sword. He uses it for protection when you seek him. Stay in my word.

"The key, you got it. The key is you. Unlock your fears, doubts, worry. Yes, you give it all to me, but you always take them back. Do I not go fast enough for you, my sweet little one? I remind you of your words again,

'Father, entwine your will with my will.' Then let it be done."

"The man with the blue-and-white gift and big smile, he brings you the cover of your book, blue and white. I gave you the name 'The Pen Will Write the Way.' This will be completed for my glory, to help my people come to know and love and trust me. So many have the same questions as you do. Help them. I have given you the gift of putting these beautiful thoughts, answers, and messages from me in a book. Complete it, little one. Forget your childhood and what you could not do. Move on, for I will always love you and be with you on this journey."

Thank you Jesus, what an incredible heart of love and compassion you have for us all. I praise you, Father, you are awesome. I am honored you chose me and I said yes.

*****

Forget the former things; do not dwell on the past. See, I am doing a new thing! Now it springs up; do you not perceive it? I am making a way in the wilderness and streams in the wasteland.

—Isaiah 43:18–19

So do not fear, for I am with you; do not
be dismayed, for I am your God. I will
strengthen you and help you; I will uphold
you with my righteous right hand.

—Isaiah 41:10

For I am the Lord your God, who takes
hold of your right hand and says to
you, Do not fear; I will help you.

—Isaiah 41:13

You make known to me the path of life, you
will fill me with joy in your presence, with
eternal pleasures at your right hand.

—Psalm 16:11

A Thankful Heart

(GUIDANCE)

Today, I will stand tall and walk with no pain because you have healed and set me free. Thank you, my Father, you have given me more names to pray for. I lift them up to you for perfect healing, and most important, they come to know your love and abide in you. I will continue to sprinkle seeds so you can continue to send the harvesters in. Thank you for all your blessings. I give you praise and thankfulness from the bottom of my heart.

Father, what word do you have for me today?

The Lord answered

"You hear my words, child, 'Be still and know I am God.' 'The truth will set you free.' I have given you

the gift of listening. Continue to listen to those in need. Be gentle in your spirit as you say my name. I am pleased you have come to terms with your fight for understanding of religion versus me. I am happy you got the message that you are not a deliverance minister but a minister of healing minds, hearts, and souls of my people by leading them to me. Keep your eyes on me, for I love you so much, little one. When it is time, you will live with me forever, but not now, child. You still have much work for me to do. I love our time together. Feel my love permeate your soul as I am feeling your love for me. Go in peace today, little one, and sprinkle seeds of my love and joy to others. Recognize the blessings I am sending you as you did yesterday, and I will send you more. Go with thankfulness and love and know I am well pleased."

How Do You See Me?

(GUIDANCE)

Father, how do you see me today?

The Lord answered

"Come, my child, come join me outside in your garden that I gave you. Hear the birds sing, see the newly cut lawn that you find so annoying when the workers come. Come see the beauty in it. They cut away all that is unnecessary so the beauty of the green grass grows healthy and brings joy to many. Go feel the cool grass beneath your feet and remember who did this for you. I have given you this beautiful home so you can be joyful. Remember, you only asked for a small bright apartment, but I chose to give you a beautiful home that will soon be fully paid for."

"Go, little one, with peace and love in your heart. Shine my light bright and cast all your cares and worries on me. My grace is sufficient for you."

"How do I see you, you ask? I see you as my beautiful child trying to fix everything and everyone. Learn, my child. I gave you this time, use it wisely. Do not love sleep. A little sleep, a little slumber, a little folding of the hands will bring poverty. Stay in my word. I live in you. Be of peace, joy, and love. Mimic me until the feelings become so strong in your heart and soul that it will be burned into your heart and soul. There will be no room for worry, fear, or doubt. You know those things are not from me. I am a God of love, kindness, patience, and mercy."

"How do I see you? I love you, little one. I see you as a beautiful flower blooming before my eyes. You are growing and blooming with love. Do not be afraid to love others or that you will do something wrong. Remember, I am guiding you. I have sent my angels to protect you and your family and those that I have entrusted in your care."

"Go, my child, walk in peace and love as I have walked in this world. This is your time to shine my light bright. Keep being thirsty for knowledge of my word. Always remember that I love you. Do not be afraid. Fear not, I reside within you, and I am with you always. Just call my name, Jesus! I am here, little one. Go in peace and love today. Cast all your cares on me. I've got this!"

Teach with Love

(GUIDANCE)

Father, help me to understand. Help me to help people, your people. Use my discerning heart to glorify you. Show me the way to heal family members and bring all my family and those you choose close to you. This is weighing heavy on my heart.

The Lord answered

"Oh, my child, you are so sensitive. I need you to be strong. It is okay to be so full of love. I walked the earth with love. There were moments I had to be strong in my words and actions, never to be hurtful because I loved so much, I wanted to heal everyone. That is your heart, sweet little one. You love so much."

"*Your mother used to tell you to toughen up and don't let people walk over you. That is not exactly what she meant. Listen to me, my child. Stay steadfast in my word. Do not be afraid for you are correct, I am mercy and love. Like a Father, I must teach you. You are a teacher. You teach with kindness and gentleness. Keep my spirit close to you. You cannot save the world. Only I can do that. Do the best you can my child. I will give you the words. Do not compare yourself with others, little one. I have made you perfect in my image. I will continue to work on your heart, wisdom, and ministry. Stay in my word. Stay steadfast. Keep learning, don't stop. Soon, it will be all clear to you. You are surrounded by wonderful people who you may not yet understand, but you will. I love you, my child. 'Keep your eyes on me, stay close to me.'*"

I love you Jesus, thank you.

Put on Your Armor

(GUIDANCE)

Father, how do you deal with the family and friends that do not understand you? I am thankful that you gave me a loving spirit, not a fighting spirit.

The Lord answered

"Oh, my child, come to me and rest. When you feel wounded, helpless, or annoyed at comments. Straighten your 'crown' stand tall and know whose daughter you are."

"Yes, it is true, they do not grasp who I am. But you, little one, must lead by faith not by sight. Do not deviate from your path. I am with you always. Do not listen to the lies that attempt to enter your head and heart. Put your shield on every morning. Armor yourself

with love. You are in a battle because of your love for me. Do not utter one word of complaint or dissatisfaction. Remember, I am the Lord, King of kings. And you, sweet one, are my child. Continue to teach your children and others. 'My grace is sufficient for you.' Show love and peace. They will recognize who I am and come to me."

*****

For we live by faith not by sight.

—Corinthians 5:7

Strength and Protection

(GUIDANCE)

Good morning, Father, I pray for the safety from devastation. Storms threaten parts of our country. I pray, Father, that it goes out to sea and causes no more damage to your people. I pray that all people lift their eyes to the heavens and see you. They seek your comfort and call out to you. Abba, Abba, Father, help them. Oh, Father, you are a God of mercy. You cannot be pleased with what is going on in the world. Bring peace to world leader's hearts.

Father, keep me strong in your love and faith. Jesus, your grace is sufficient for me.

The Lord answered

"You are my flower, you bloom for me. Perhaps someday, you will grace me with your fragrance."

I give thanks to you for this day. I give thanks to you for protection over my family. I give thanks to you for protection for our great country. I give thanks to you for the healing.

You are a God of love and mercy. I will teach my family to follow you. Thank you, Father, for your teachings, your love, and your faithfulness.

Jesus, how do you see me today?

The Lord answered

"You are still trying too hard. My yoke is light and easy. You say you want to walk the earth like me. Where in the Bible and the words I have given you do you see worry? When did you see me not forgive? You see me in peace, you see me heal the sick. It was not by my might but by my Father. You want to be like me, and then go heal the sick, spread healing words over them. Go peacefully and give all your worries to me. Go love everyone, even those that hurt you. Walk in faith and know that I am God."

"Your dream last night when you were in a building, you saw a family member smiling. You were safe. There was a fear that people would see blood on your clothes. Search your heart, my child, do not be intimidated or hesitant to speak my name. You were in a state of anxiety, fear, and doubt that plague you that your family will be cast out. Shut it down and the door will be closed, never to assault you again."

"The door to enter the building or leave was protected by guards. I have sent my angels as a barrier to protect you and your family. Do you see that little one?"

Yes I do, Jesus, thank you. I give you all praise and thanks, sweet Jesus.

"Be strong, my child, for I love you. You are beginning to truly understand my ways. I will wrap my arms around you and your family that I have entrusted you to care for. Hide under my wings and be safe. Actually, you are not hiding but taking comfort in me by coming to me for protection."

"'Do you think I cannot call on my Father, and he will at once put at my disposal more than twelve legions of angels?' (Matthew 26:53).

"So you see, my child, there it is again, the number 12. I send twelve legions of angels to surround you and your family and those you love. Go in peace and comfort today and know that 'peace be still for I am God.'

"I love you my child and I am thankful for the work you are doing for me."

*****

Later Jesus found him at the temple and said
to him "See, you are well again. Stop sinning
or something worse may happen to you." The
man went away and told the Jewish leaders
that it was Jesus who had made him well.

—John5:14–15

Quickening Spirit

(GUIDANCE)

Good morning, my sweet, wonderful Father, Counselor, and Lover of my soul. Once again, I am privileged to sit and meet here with you in the garden. The peace, tranquility, and your presence bring such joy to my heart.

It's a new day, Father. The trees are beginning to turn color, leaves falling one by one. They are dying and falling to the ground. There will be a new birth in spring, when they will become green, beautiful, and will provide shade. Their roots reach deep into the ground, and they will weather storms, wind, rain, and the snow of winter. They will remain strong and stand tall. Some whose roots do not reach deep into the ground and steadfast will fall to the wind. Father, I want my roots to be so deep in you that I will weather the storm. I put my trust in you, sweet Jesus, for with you, everything is possible.

Oh, my Great Counselor, you are teaching me every day is a new day filled with your love, grace, and mercy. I can and will be joyful and weather the storms of life. Sweet Jesus, you once told me I was in a metamorphosis for you. You saw me struggling for I had taken my eyes off you. I have so many questions today. I ask for your guidance that I recognize and hear your voice. I have been told by another to ask that you quicken my spirit and give me divine acceleration.

Like the leaves that fall from the tree that awaits a new birth, every day is a new day. When I awake, I am alive in you and you in me. I will walk in your grace, mercy, and love. Sweet Jesus, we are here together blessed in this beautiful garden. Please whisper in my ear the desires of your heart for me.

The Lord answered

"Oh, my child, you bring such joy to my heart. Your childlike innocence is what I desire and love to see. I know your love for me. Quicken your spirit, you ask? Okay, little one, hang on. I said it before, and I will say it again: you are in for the ride of your life. Behold, I am

doing something new. Continue to feel my joy, my love, my presence. Listen closely to the guidance of the Holy Spirit. Be anxious for nothing as I am leading the way."

"I once gave you a dream of a carriage driven by a unicorn[1] in the middle with a white horse on each side. You are in the carriage, child. You are being led by my Father, the Son, and the Holy Spirit. You have heard it said, 'Can you get a more powerful combination than that—the Father, the Son, and the Holy Spirit—guiding you?' Oh, little one, you are so loved. Finally, you are going to feel what true love for you feels like. You are now able to walk in true love and give to others."

"A quickening spirit! Take heed, child, and seek guidance from the Holy Spirit. Soon, I will be putting the finishing touches on the beautiful butterfly you are becoming for my kingdom, my glory. The kingdom you will live in with me."

---

1   Author's note: When looking up the definition of a *unicorn*, it was found to have three accepted meanings

1.   A single horned horse like mythical animal
2.   A start-up company valued at one billion dollars in the software or technology industry
3.   A carriage driven by three horses with one leader

My interpretation: the Father, the Son, and the Holy Spirit.

"Go in love in your heart and know I am well pleased with your desire to walk the earth as I did. I love you, little one."

Oh, how I love you, sweet Jesus, Lover of my soul. As I watch the leaves fall, I look forward to the rebirth of spring. I look forward to my rebirth each morning upon awakening. What an awesome God we serve.

*****

I can do all this through him
who gives me strength.

—Philippians4:13

But when the kindness and love of God our Savior
appeared, he saved us, not because of righteous
things we had done, but because of his mercy.
He saved us through the washing, of rebirth and
renewal by the Holy Spirit, whom he poured out
on us generously through Jesus Christ our Savior.

—Titus3:4–6

THE PEN WILL WRITE THE WAY

See I am doing a new thing! Now it springs up;
do you not perceive it? I am making a way in
the wilderness and streams in the wasteland.

—Isaiah43:19

The Power of God's Protection

(GUIDANCE)

Good morning, my faithful Father. The garden is absolutely beautiful this morning. There is not a breeze in the air, just the warmth of the sun. I feel your presence so strongly this morning. I hear your voice, I feel your peace. I see you smile—I even hear you laugh. These are indeed the sounds of joy. How can anyone be sad in your presence? The joy you share with me in the garden cannot be surpassed by anyone or anything. It's only with you, my sweet Jesus, Lover of my soul.

My thoughts wander to past experiences. How did I come to be in this place of peace and love I am in today? I see your hand. I see when you saved me from making mistakes. I see when you took my hand and pulled me up and out of that dark place to safety. I am so thankful for the beautiful gifts of family, friends, good health, and enough finances to live a comfortable life. The garden is such a beautiful gift. The peace, the comfort, your presence—what more could anyone ask for? Father, each morning, you teach me a lesson. I come to you with repentance for the sins I have committed against you and the sins I do not recognize. I come to you with a humble heart, and I ask, sweet Jesus, what lesson would you like to teach me this morning?

The Lord answered

"Look to the left on the deck. See the lifeless slug? It is so very fragile. It once lived. Now, it lies there lifeless as you can see it was very delicate. It lacks a shell for protection, so it became vulnerable to the environment. Without a shell, he met his fate."

"Little one, though you do not have a shell that appears hard and indestructible, I have given you clear instruction to put on your armor from your feet to your head. You are my child, little one, you are a warrior for me. You and your loved ones are under my protection. Now, harden your shell and stop allowing doubt to come back. You conquered it, child! Keep your words and thoughts safe. Live it, walk it, believe you are a child of

God, a woman of faith, a warrior for me. You are my precious warrior. Cast out doubt as it is not from me. I love you, little one."

I love you, sweet Jesus. I will wear the armor of God proudly, for I am your warrior, the daughter of the Most High God, King of kings, Lord of lords.

*****

When the Angel of the Lord appeared to Gideon, he said, "The Lord is with you mighty warrior."

—Judges 6:12

Summer Coming to a Close

(GUIDANCE)

Good morning, Father. We are coming to the close of summer. It is raining here in the garden. I placed a bright pinwheel here in the garden to remind me of your teaching to stop going around and around in circles and to jump into your loving arms and you will catch me. Sweet Jesus, you are such an awesome loving, caring, and teaching God. I feel so blessed to have you in my life.

Soon, the children will be back in school. Four of my own grandchildren are going off to college, the two little ones climbing the ladder. Some children are excited, some leery, some confused and anxious, and some embracing their new lives and experiences. The same goes for their parents. Some are excited to let them go, some are sad the children (who are now young adults) that they have nurtured grow up and

49

leave the nest. The empty-nest syndrome is what it is called.

What word of encouragement would you give to all today?

The Lord answered

"Aah, my child, the art of letting go and letting me, God, watch over them. Know it is both an exciting time for some and for others, a fearful time. They have fear of not achieving, fear of not making the right decisions, fear of finances for costly schools. Help them turn their fear into faith by trusting me. Your society is filled with negative ideas pounded into not only children's minds but adults as well. The children are exposed to unhealthy video games, bullying, instant gratification, and unkindness to others. The adults are exposed to movies filled with violence, politics with different views, not respecting each other, the media with false teachings and disrespect for the American flag and the president of your great country."

"Are you strong enough? Did you teach your children to be strong and replace negative thoughts with positive words? What are you feeding your children spir-

itually? Are you teaching them to come to me when they are weary?"

"The ways of this world are not my ways. Are you teaching them to replace worry and fear with my name? Are you teaching them to call on me? I am teaching you to go teach others. You can do this for me. Tell my people how much I love them."

I will tell them. Thank you, Father. Today, I will go with a thankful heart and pray for our children, their parents, and our great nation.

*****

For we live by faith, not by sight.

—2 Corinthians5:7

I can do all this through him who gives me strength.

—Philippians 4:13

God Reveals a Dream

(GUIDANCE)

Good morning, sweet Jesus. On this cool damp day, I can sit and look out at the garden, thankful knowing you are here with me now. Thank you for choosing me to follow you. Thankful for all you are teaching me. Oh, my wonderful counselor, I see you, feel you. My spirit rejoices in you, my God, my Lord, my Savior. Father, today, you revealed a dream you have given me twice in my lifetime. I am forever grateful and thankful. I praise your holy name.

Many years ago, when I was a child of perhaps eight or ten years old, I had a dream. I see it in my mind's eye so clearly. I was standing outside of the home we lived in. I see the house, I see myself on the sidewalk looking up to the sky. There was a ladder appearing to reach into the sky going beyond the clouds. I tried to climb the ladder, but to no avail.

There was a beautiful light in the sky. It was the sun. The sky was bright blue, the clouds white, with an endless ladder that I could not climb. I did not think much about it, nor did I share it with anyone.

About two years ago, I had another dream. I was asleep in my bed. I saw my room so clearly. There it was again, the endless ladder reaching into the bright sky. I saw myself once again, reaching for the ladder. I could not climb it. I turned to look at my bed. I was sleeping. I saw myself asleep in my bed, but I was not. I was trying to climb the ladder. I remember waking and asking what had just happened. Did I have an out-of-body experience? I once mentioned this dream to someone. He called it Jacob's ladder. Today, you placed it on my heart to search the meaning of this ladder. I found it in Genesis 28:12. Sweet Jesus, why do you bring this dream to me now?

The Lord answered

"You are learning, my child. Your mind is like a memory bank, storing all the information I am giving to you now and through the years. Only now I am pleased that you are writing and recording what I am showing you. Oh yes, little one, you have loved me even as a child,

and I knew your love for me. I have always loved you. Your childhood desire to become a nun and serve me was duly noted. However, I had and have a better plan for your life. I have given you a beautiful family. You see, child, I need you to teach and make disciples of them all. They will go out into the world and work for me in their own way. They will help others and bring them to me. You seek my word, child. You are growing up in me. You are learning at a quicker pace. You asked me to quicken your spirit, and so I am. Once again, I say I am pleased with your work and love our encounters in the morning. Oh, the dreams, child, I am revealing them to you because you are now open to hear my voice and my teachings."

"The ladder—Jacob's ladder, as it is called—you searched my word until you found it. This makes me smile. Your desire to learn about angels pleases me. Your questions are being answered. I know you do not want to put idols, even angels, before me. I am pleased you are looking into the spirit world and seeking answers. Yesterday, when you felt a breeze pass you inside a room where there would be no breeze, and then again around your feet, they are my angels assigned to protect you. You recognized them and were thankful to not only them but most importantly me."

"Last week, you were driving and almost crashed into a median. An angel took your wheel and quickly turned it so you missed the median. What was it that you asked? 'I did not turn the wheel that sharp,' you replied. Then you thanked me and the angel I sent to save you from the accident. Your family chuckles and feels safe with you driving because they recognize that you drive with angels. Once more, you had your youngest grandchildren in the car. You always pray when you drive especially with your 'precious cargo,' as you call them. You almost swerved into the left lane, and once again, you were protected. You shouted out, 'Thank you, Jesus.' You called my name. You then heard a sweet voice from the back seat from the youngest child. He asked, 'Gram, can I invite Jesus into my life?' You replied, 'Sure, but why did you ask?' He answered, 'Because I want him to protect me.' When you got to a quiet place, you prayed with him. When he got home, he told his mother and dad with great excitement, 'Jesus is in me!' Oh, my child, you are doing my work. You do not recognize the work you do because of your humbleness. I love your heart for me, little one. I love you. Go walk in peace and worry not. When the time is here, you will climb the ladder to heaven escorted by my beautiful angels I have assigned to you. Keep learning, keep growing, and keep *walking in love. You are mine, child, and I will be with you for all eternity."*

Thank you, Jesus, for not only your love, your faithfulness, but for the daunting task and price you paid not only for the sins of the world but for me. I love you, and I am encountering your peace, grace, and your empowering mercy. I love you, Father.

*****

He had a dream, in which he saw a stairway resting on the earth, with its top reaching heaven, and the angels of God were ascending and descending on it. There above it stood the Lord, and he said: "I am the Lord, the God of your father Abraham and the God of Isaac. I will give you and your descendants the land on which you are lying. Your descendants will be like the dust of the earth, and you will spread out to the west and to the east, to the north and to the south. All peoples on earth will be blessed through your offspring. I am with you and will watch over you wherever you go, and I will bring you back to this land. I will not leave you until I have done what I promised you.

—Genesis28:12–15

Teach Me Father, Please

(G̲UIDANCE)

Good morning Jesus. Oh, my Father, I feel such joy in my heart as I sit here in the garden with you this morning. There is so much for me to do, my morning began feeling overwhelmed and tired. But you, sweet Jesus restored my energy, thank you for this blessing. I am excited to go to Church and praise and worship you today. It is indeed a glorious morning here in the garden. The combination of the quiet, the greenery, the trees and flowers in full bloom, the sun's warmth over my body and singing birds bring such joy and peace to my heart.

I come to you with a thankful heart for the gentle work you are doing not only in me but my family. Oh how blessed I am to be able to sit here with you in this lovely garden.

Sweet Jesus, what will you teach me through nature today?

The Lord answered:

"Little one, look at the large tree to the right, straight ahead of you. See where I am standing? Now, look closely at the tree, there are hardly any leaves towards the bottom, they are small and sparse. Now, look towards the top of the tree, they begin to grow larger. Now child, look at the top of the tree, it is full of leaves, bright green and large.

Think of the tree as my children. Some just stay on the bottom, they do not seek me, they do not come to me, they do not grow. They remain stagnant, some never grow. The leaves attempting to reach the top are growing slowly but they are growing. Now, look at the top of the tree it is full, the leaves are bright and green. It is crowded up there. These are the children seeking the sun. These are the children looking to the heavens. These represent the children reaching for the sky, reaching for me. These leaves represent the children climbing, praying, seeking, searching my word, seeking me just as you do little one, each morning you spend time praising and worshiping me, seeking my word. You learn to become more peaceful.

Yes, my child you will grow like the top of that tree full of my wisdom, grace and mercy. I love you little one, keep your eyes on me, stay in the state of peace as it gives me much joy. Now go to church and hear the word I have for you today."

Thank you Jesus, I love you!

*****

"But blessed is the man who trusts in the Lord, whose confidence is in him. He will be like a tree planted by the water that sends out its roots by the stream. It does not fear when heat comes; its leaves are always green. It has no worries in a year of drought and never fails to bear fruit.

Jeremiah 17:7-8

He is like a tree planted by streams of water, which yields its fruit in season and whose leaf does not wither. Whatever he does prospers

Psalm 1:3

The joy of the Lord is my strength

Nehemiah 8:10

Calm the Sea of Your Life

(WORRY)

Oh, Lord, come to me this morning, my heart is heavy. Help me to help my family. Help me to help myself. So many questions I have, so many concerns. How do you see me today Father?

The Lord answered

"Come to me so I can give you rest, my child. The ocean waves are sometimes strong and turbulent, but I can calm the seas. You are in a turbulent wave right now, but my grace is sufficient for you. Let my love permeate your soul. I am here. I will calm the sea of your life. Ride the wave little one. Ride it and hold on to the sunny shore that awaits you. Your answers will come."

"Trust and believe!"

"For I know the plans I have for you", declares the Lord, "plans to prosper you and not to harm you, plans to give you hope and a future. Then you will call on me and come and pray to me, and I will listen to you. You will seek me and find me when you seek me with all your heart. I will be found by you," declares the Lord, "and will bring you back from captivity. I will gather you from all the nations and places where I have banished you," declares the Lord," and I will bring you back to the place from which I carried you into exile." (Jeremiah 29:11–14)

*****

"Walk by faith little one, not by sight. I am here and I will never leave your side. Trust and believe I am taking care of your family."

Bring Cheer

(WORRY)

Holy Spirit, what would you like to say to me today?

The Lord answered

"Do not worry about tomorrow, for tomorrow brings worry of its own. Walk with me in faith, my child. Stay steadfast in your work and thoughts. Stay strong. I am with you, I will never leave you. I will hold you with my victorious right hand. Go today with a smile on your face, God in your in your heart, and be of love. Smile love on all those around you. Do not be of little cheer. Be of great cheer. Focus on me. Keep your eyes on me. Do not worry about your family. Remove *fear on your heart. Follow me, child, and I will lead you to victory."*

*****

Thank you, Jesus, for today, I will enjoy the precious present.

God's Protective Bubble

(DOUBT)

Come to me, Father, please. Help me to recognize your will for my life. Father, what do you want me to speak into my life at this time? Help me please. Transform my mind, my heart, and my soul into your kind and gentle way.

The Lord answered

"Why are you so troubled, child? Do you not believe I am who I say I am? I know your heart, I know your doubts, I know your fears. Fear not, I am with you. Stop trying so hard. Thinker! You are such a thinker. See the birds in the sky now? They do not worry. Give all your worries to me, child, I know your heart. You are growing beautifully. I know your love for me. I know

you believe I am who I say I am. Do not listen to the lies. They are doubt and fear. I will help you overcome. I know you know they are not from me. Focus more on me. Stop worrying about correct scripture. You had it in the beginning, and you still have it. Bring it back! My peace, mercy, my grace are sufficient for you. Fear not, my child. I will hold you with my victorious right hand. My love for you will prevail. Picture yourself and your loved ones and all you love in a bubble. This is my promise: the bubble of my protection covered with my blood I have shed for you and those you love. There is room, child, there is room for more to come into this bubble. You may well lead them to me. You picked up on Kathy Lee's words: 'If I had the cure for cancer, would I keep it to myself?' Well, I have the cure for the malignancy of your soul. His name is Jesus. I urge you to speak it to all you are prompted to. Go in peace, live in joy. That is what is pleasing to me. Calm your mind and let my love in and permeate your soul. You are okay, little one. You are on the track for greatness for my kingdom. Remember, I have chosen you, and you said, 'Yes, Lord, yes!'

"Peace be with you and allow me to do my work in you. Look up, child, keep your eyes on me."

*****

For those who are led by the Spirit of God are
the children of God. The Spirit you received
does not make you slaves, so that you live
in fear again; rather, the Spirit you received
brought about your adoption to sonship.
And by him we cry, "Abba, Father."

—Romans 8:14–15

A Forgiving Heart

(FORGIVENESS)

Good morning Father. My heart has been in turmoil. Fight against principalities? I am not a fighter, Lord. I am a lover, and you are my best lover. You have given me the authority and covered me in your precious blood to cast out the enemy. Father, teach me to pray the way you would pray. Teach me to walk as you walked the earth. Fight, Father? What need do I have to fight when I can pray to you? You have given me the great counselor, the Holy Spirit. For this gift, I am grateful and come to you with a humble heart. My heart, eyes, and ears are open to your voice, sweet Jesus. The table, Father, what message would you like to teach me about the broken glass tabletop? Teach me please.

The Lord answered

"Good morning, my child. I love our time together in the morning. The sun shines bright. I sent you a little rabbit to say hello. You are learning your lessons well, little one. You can now see what transpires when you take your eyes off me. Yes, it is true, Satan comes to kill, steal, and destroy your peace. I am pleased you rebuke and bring your focus and eyes of your heart back to me. The table, little one, yes you are correct. There is a message in it for you. Through carelessness, you dropped the glass and broke the corner of your glass table. Eventually, the table will weaken, and glass will shatter. The break will destroy the entire glass. Do not allow that to happen to you, my child. A piece of your heart was broken with confrontation from dear friends. Forgive and help them to understand in your own gentle way. I can and will restore the broken piece of your heart unlike the glass that cannot be restored. You have chosen to come to me, seek my forgiveness for allowing your joy to be stolen by the enemy. It is a learning process, little one. Stay steadfast in my word. Pray as you always pray with your heart. Keep your focus on me, for I am the truth, the way, and the life. Go in peace with love in your heart. Shine your light bright and speak my name. Lead by *example, not pressure or preaching. I love you, little one, and am pleased you continue your work for me."*

So now I understand, Father. The corner of the glass broke, and left that way, the break in the glass will spread and shatter and be completely destroyed. So it is with unforgiveness in our heart and soul. If we do not forgive, our heart becomes hardened, our soul becomes darkened, and we lose our joy. Our joy gets replaced with bitterness, resentment, and anger. Though this was an expensive lesson, I thank you, Lord, for it was only a piece of glass. It was truly a valuable lesson on forgiveness.

Father your grace is sufficient for me. Your love, grace, and mercy prevails above all others.

Metamorphosis

(LOVE)

Good morning, Father, my sweet Jesus. Here we are again this morning. The sun shines bright, the warmth brings comfort to my soul. You have sent the lovely birds to sing to me this morning. How green and beautiful the grass and trees and all that surround me are. Thank you, Jesus.

Father, you once showed me a butterfly. You told me I was in a metamorphosis for you. Here I am, Lord. Change and transform my mind, my heart, my body to become all that you desire me to be for your glory. This is my desire, Lord. Let me lead your people to victory through your salvation. Feel my love as I place myself on the altar for you. Slip a needle of love into my heart, sweet Jesus. My struggles are real. My love for you is growing stronger and deeper. I love that you are the Lover of my soul. I love how you send comforters to me when I am down on myself. I thank you, Lord, for the new people in my life. I thank you for my mentor, Harry, whose words of encouragement, wisdom, and teachings brings me peace. His words changed my life. They were "He is your best lover, let him have his way."

Father, tell me what you see as I progress in this metamorphosis for you?

The Lord answered

"I see you still struggling, child. You have allowed your mind to control your body, your thoughts. You have taken your eyes off me even though consciously, you do not mean to. You have allowed worry, the pain in your back to become your idol. You have bogged down your mind with teachings that were meant to show you that my perfect love casts out all fear. It is okay, little one, you are learning and growing. I love how you continue to seek me and hear my voice. Stay on your path, you do hear my voice. Now feel my love as you did in your dream, for it was not a dream. It was I, child, wrapping my loving arms around you. It was just a glimpse of the future I have planned for you. How do I see you in this metamorphosis? You are about to break out, little one.

You are about to become the most beautiful soul I intend you to be. However, I have given you a strategy before, child. Take heed and implement it now. Wait no longer! Eat properly, rest, and keep your eyes on me. Do not tire, or you will become vulnerable to the prey of the enemy. You have said it before, 'Father, I give my will to you, entwine your will with mine." Then let it be, little one. Allow my love to fill you up and permeate your soul. I am here, child. I am with you on this beautiful journey called life."

Thank you, Jesus, I am in awe of your faithfulness, love, grace, and mercy for me. I do have faith as tiny as a mustard seed. It is about to grow, and I will move that mountain.

*****

Jesus turned and saw her. "Take heart daughter", he said, "your faith has healed you." And the woman was healed at that moment.

—Matthew 9:22

He replied, "Because you have so little faith. Truly I tell you, if you have faith as small as a mustard seed, you can say to this mountain, 'Move from here to there,' and it will move.' Nothing is impossible for you."

—Matthew 17:20

Searching for God's Love

(LOVE)

God sent me a dream. In this dream was an arm with a hand like a fist that appeared to be searching from the sea like a periscope from a submarine coming up from the sea to the top of the water. I asked you, Father, "What does this mean?"

The Lord answered

"As in a periscope, you are searching for my love child."

I replied, "Father, I was searching for your love. I was searching for your relentless pursuit of affection from me and mine for you. Father, you are here now. I have your love. I no longer need to search for it. What I do need is to feel your love more and more

74

and to bring it to those hurting and to those in need of hearing your voice. To help them feel your love as I love and feel you in my heart."

The Lord answered

"Yes, child, you understand. Stay on your path. The greatest gift I give you is love. The greatest gift you give to others is love. In this difficult world, it becomes challenging to remain in the state of love, and that is why I ask, keep your eyes on me. Little one, keep your eyes on Jesus."

"Your world is full of distractions and interruptions. Do rebuke the spirit of distractions in my name. The name Jesus will always prevail. I love you, little one, my darling child."

What Is Agape Love?

(LOVE)

Agape (uh-gah-pay) love is God's love. The Greek word *agape* means "Love is unconditional, selfless giving of God, to meet our need." It is unconditional, selfless giving of love from us to meet the needs of others.

Father, show me how to love in this moment of pain, chaos, and turmoil in loved ones. Challenges are coming against me. How do I stay in Agape love?

You, sweet Jesus, are wanting to restore my peace, my health, my finances—not only in myself but all those that surround me with the same concerns. Heal my aching heart with your agape love. Father, you walked the earth with unconditional love and forgiveness. It is taught that agape love has an unrelenting reach, a love that never stops giving and never stops forgiving. Wow, this is so powerful! Father, I want this kind of love. My desire has always been to walk the earth like you did. Now, I have a clear understanding of how you loved with agape love. I know it is mine for the asking. This morning, I come again with a humble heart, asking that seed of love you placed in my heart guide me. Teach me how to water these seeds. Make it grow into your agape love. Give me the wisdom, courage to both love and forgive, and bring forth the light to those who live in despair, darkness, anger, and hurt. Those who feel rejected, those searching for love in all the wrong places. There is only one place to find love, sweet Jesus, it is in you! I pray that I may go out today and be bold for you, Jesus, my Lord and Savior.

Father, again, I ask, please teach me to love with agape love. Give me wisdom to help all those in need. Give me the strength of the Lion of Judah.

The Lord answered

"'Oh child, ye of little faith, be still and know that I am God.' You have asked me to slip a needle of faith and love in your heart, and so I did. It is there, little one, now allow it to grow. Your biggest obstacle is you, your thoughts. You lack agape love for yourself. Love yourself before you can give love to others. Forgive yourself for

your own inequities so that you can forgive others. You are strong, you are courageous. Do not listen to the lies. Replace them with my name. Do not be afraid to call on me. Say my name, for I am with you always, child. Do not sway like a tree that falls in the wind. It sways left to right, whichever way the wind takes it. You, my child, must be like a tree planted by the water that sends out its roots by the stream. It does not fear when heat comes, its leaves are always green. It has no worries in a year of drought and never fails to bear fruit. Worry not, my child. Hear my voice as I am taking care of your family. I will heal the sick, for it has already been done. Trust and believe. Now, go with agape love in your heart. And once again, I say, 'Be still and know I am God,' for I will always love you little one."

Oh, how I love you, sweet Jesus, you are my right hand. Thank you for filling me up with your agape love. Today, I will stand tall, straighten my crown because I am the child of the Most High King of kings and Lord of lords. Father, your grace is sufficient for me.

*****

He says, "Be still, and know that I am
God, I will be exalted among nations,
I will be exalted in the earth."

—Psalm 46:10

But blessed is the one who trusts in the Lord,
whose confidence is in him. They will be like a
tree planted by the water that sends out its roots
by the stream. It does not fear when heat comes;
its leaves are always green. It has no worries in a
year of drought and never fails to bear fruit.

—Jeremiah 17:7–8

Be Anxious for Nothing

(TRUST)

Good morning, Father. Many years ago, you gave me a dream. I, along with my two daughters, were walking through what appeared to be a dark cave. One child on my left has a doll dangling from her hand. The second child on my right is holding my hand. As we walked through this dark cave, there were people on the right and left of us who appeared to be unhappy and troubled. We were being led out by a young handsome man dressed in a white gown, like Jesus would wear. He was leading us out to safety into the light. The child holding the doll was asked to give it up, but she would not let it go. The young man would continue to lead us to safety. The light appeared at the end of the cave. We were out of the darkness into the light. We were safe. I remember looking for my father. Or was I looking for my Heavenly Father, Jesus? The handsome young man disappeared. We were left in the light of day on a busy street with cars and people. We were led to safety just as Jesus promises. Father, tell me, please, more about the meaning of this dream?

The Lord answered

"Child, you always tell people that there is light at the end of the tunnel. You sometimes take the wisdom I have given you for granted. You take it lightly, and then one day, you get the magnitude of my messages and dreams and understand them. You had yet another dream in a dark place as if a tunnel. Again, with your daughters, but one had blood on her clothing. You were all covered in the blood of my protection I shed for you. The entrance was protected for you and your family by my angels. They were placed there to guard your safety. Yes, little one, it was I leading you through the darkness and misery of those around you. The doll—sometimes we do not want to let things go. We hold on to things, almost making them idols in your lives. You were led to safety. You were led into the light by me, for 'I am the truth, the way and the life.' Let no idols come before me. You were looking for your father when you came out of *the darkness into the light. You were seeking me, child, your Heavenly Father. As you looked around, the young man disappeared. But it was I, child. I will never disappear. I live in you always. I am in your heart and soul. I will protect you always. Once again, I say, 'Keep your eyes on me, keep your eyes on Jesus.' I know your heart, I know your pain, I know you're hurt. Yet it reminds me of another dream I have given you. Things will come up in your life, give them to me. I am your right hand. Trust and believe and be thankful. Give all your worries to me, child, with thanksgiving in your heart. I have you and your loved ones in the palm of my hands. Go in peace today and never forget, your joy brings me great joy! I love you, little one."*

*****

Do not be anxious about anything, but in every situation, by prayer and petition, with thanksgiving, present your requests to God. And the peace of God, which transcends all understanding, will guard your hearts and your minds in Jesus Christ.

—Philippians 4:6–7

THE PEN WILL WRITE THE WAY

You make your saving help my shield, and
your right hand sustains me; your help has
made me great. You provide a broad path for
my feet, so that my ankles do not give way.

—Psalm 18:35–36

Cluttered House, Cluttered Mind, Cluttered Body

(CHANGE)

Good morning Father, Memorial Day is upon us. It is raining, and a peaceful rain it is. The earth is soaking up every drop, saying feed me now, feed my thirst. Saturate my ground, for I know there will be a dry spell. Just as there are dry spells in our lives. Sometimes, we feel stuck and at a standstill. Things are not moving as quickly or as purposely as we would like them to. Father, why do we stifle ourselves? Why do we get stuck on our path? Why do we have dry spells?

Walking on God's Path

(TEACHING)

Good morning, Father. The garden is still wet from the rain, but the sun shines bright. "Go walk on the wet grass," I heard you say. "Sit on the bench and soak with me in the sun." And so I did. I did for my desire is to be obedient to the Holy Spirit.

Yes, it is sunny and dry on the bench. The wet grass beneath my feet tickles me to awaken my spirit. As you know, Father, I had an evening of anxiety once again. I gave into worry and lack of faith in you, even when knowing you are taking care of all life's circumstances. Once again, I give all my concerns up to you. As I write this, the pinwheel in my neighbor's garden is spinning around and around in circles. It just stopped. I heard you say, "Yes child, I heard your cries. The pinwheel signifies you going around in circles, and you jumped off the wheel into my loving arms."

Sweet Jesus, as I go back and read our morning encounters, I find myself repetitive. I ask you the same questions over and over again. You are always so gracious to answer me: "Be still and know that I am God."

I repent for my sin of lack of faith. I know you know that I have faith as tiny as a mustard seed. Once again, I come to you with a humble heart and ask, please, sweet Jesus, impart your ways on me. This is my desire to worship and honor you with complete thankfulness in my heart.

The Lord answered

"Oh, my child, I am pleased you were obedient to my voice and came to sit with me on the bench. I know how much you love the sun as it beats gently on your heart for me. It warms your entire being and brings you peace and tranquility to be open to hear what I will teach you this morning."

"Your view is a little different sitting here on the bench with me, but you still enjoy the beauty of the gifts I have given you. I love your thankfulness, child. Perhaps

we should look at things differently—a different perspective, shall we say. Now look at the path ahead and study it. Do you see that it does not go straight? Follow it with your eyes. Sometimes, it veers to the left, and sometimes it veers to the right. Then at the end of the path, you have a choice. You can make a left turn or a right turn, but you are still on the path. Sometimes, child, we choose the wrong turn. We stay on the path, but it is not always filled with my desires for you. You look and say, 'I should have gone right.' That is the direction I need you to go to find the way to my destination. I told you before, stay on your path and keep your eyes on me. I am the fruit of the spirit. The fruit of the spirit is peace, patience, kindness, goodness, faithfulness, gentleness, and self-control. Against such things, there is no law" (Galatians 5:22–23).

"As you taught your family, life is about learning lessons. As long as you keep your eyes on me and come to me when you are weary, you will stay on the path I have set before you. Like the colony of ants that travel in a straight line, one goes astray but gently gets nudged back into line. When you detour from the path I have set before you, I will bring you back to me, for I am a gentle, loving, and forgiving God. Go in peace today and stay steadfast in my word. Now go enjoy the precious present, for this is my gift to you and your loved ones.

This is a gift I give to all who accept the seed you have planted in their hearts."

Thank you, Jesus, your grace is sufficient for me. I will walk in peace and love today. You are an incredible teacher, sweet Jesus. I will walk the path you have set before me with thankfulness in my heart.

*****

Do not be anxious about anything but in every situation, by prayer and petition, with thanksgiving, present your requests to God.

—Philippians 4:6

I can do all this through him who gives me strength.

—Philippians 4:13

Finding Answers in Our Heart and Soul

(TEACHING)

Good morning, dear sweet Jesus.

I sit here in total amazement of the gifts you are waiting to bestow on us just for the asking. I see in my mind's eye so many beautiful gifts wrapped in shiny gold paper. Some wrapped in silver paper with beautiful bows. Some more of the gifts wrapped in blue. It is a known fact that man searches the earth for precious gold and diamonds by digging and mining. It is indeed a difficult task. If we would only dig deep in the mines of our hearts and souls, we shall find the riches of love, peace, joy, and the mercy that you, sweet Jesus, promise and desire so desperately to bestow upon us. Father, why is it that so few dig deep into the hidden treasures of our hearts and souls? Why is it that only a few receive your beautiful gifts?

The Lord answered

"Time, little one, it takes time. So many people do not want to take the time to spend with me, reading my words as they are written in the Bible, learning to recognize and hear my voice. You live in an 'I want it now' world, a world that everyone wants instant gratification. It is easier for them to search for their riches in lotto tickets, gambling, food, and whatever else their addictions are to fill their emptiness and instant gratification. You, my child, are learning to come to me so I can give you rest and the desires of your heart. My peace and riches are not found in a church pew or religion or any of the worldly desires that have been sold through false teachings. As you are learning, it takes time to read, to seek, as in Matthew 7:7: 'Seek and you shall find.' I, your Father, receive such joy in your joy. This is a gift available to everyone. Teach them it is necessary to spend time in my word. They need to keep their eyes on me. The human mind is so incredible and has the capacity to learn so much. Instead of filling it with my teachings, they choose to fill their minds with unbelief, fear, and doubt. They are being fed the

lies of the enemy through movies, books, television, and false teachings. Little one, it is my job to save the world, not yours. All I ask, once again, is sprinkle your seeds by example of love and peace in your heart. Your career is sales. You do not have to sell me child."

"Just show me as you would show the finest diamond. Show my people the benefits of my wisdom, love, and most of all, my peace and mercy. I give to those who come to me to live a life of eternity this way. Who would refuse it? If they do, it is not your job to badger them to love me, to accept me as their Lord and Savior. It is a choice, but if you do not sprinkle seeds and open your mouth, they may miss it. Open your mouth, and I will fill it. Now go in peace and spread love."

I understand, Father, the key word is *time*. "Take time before time takes you." There is no price tag we can put on the time we spend with you, sweet Jesus, for you are so worthy. Worthy is the lamb.

*****

Ask and it will be given to you;
seek and you will find; knock and the
door will be opened to you.

—Matthew 7:7

You will seek me and find me when
you seek me with all your heart.

—Jeremiah 29:13

"Come to me, all who are weary and burdened,
and I will give you rest. Take my yoke upon you
and learn from me, for I am gentle and humble
in heart, and you will find rest for your souls.
For my yoke is easy and my burden is light."

—Matthew 11:28–30

Spread Wisdom

(TEACHING)

The world is sleeping. The celebration of a new year comes forth. I have so much to be thankful for, my Father, even the trials and tribulations can be used for my teaching and growth. I am ready to step up to the next level to be used for your glory. Teach me, Father, in your kindly way. I want to be a vessel to bring forth your love and mercy. Help me to teach not only my family but those who are willing to learn the wonders of your love and compassion for them. Help me to bring forth and teach your voice to all those open to hear it. I love you, sweet Jesus. I relinquish my will to you. Entwine your will with mine so I walk in total confidence with no doubt or fear, my merciful and loving God.

How do you see me today, Father? What would you like to say to me?

<u>The Lord answered</u>

"Keep your eyes on me, child. Do not deviate from your path. I know how hard you have worked to get where you are today. I have blessed you with wisdom, a kind heart, and love. This New Year will bring many blessings to you. Yes, there will always be challenges. Put your armor on daily, for I have sent a legion of angels to protect you and your family. Worry no more. Your faith in me will suffice and bring you to where you need to be to teach others. Go forward with your plans. Your desire to teach others how to hear my voice will lead the way. Remember the words Harry told you last December, 'He is your best lover, let him have his way.' Do not fear your weakness, for it is the stage on which my power and glory perform most brilliantly. You are learning, my child. You are a soldier in my army, for that I am well pleased. Go forth with love in your heart and stop trying to be perfect, for it is I, the righteous one. Repent and always remember, you are covered in my blood. I love you, child. Remember my words: 'Your joy is my joy, let the pen write the way.'"

A Seed Sprinkler

(TEACHING)

Good morning, Father, I come to the garden alone while the dew is still on the roses. What a beautiful heartfelt song it is, and it plays over and over again in my mind and heart. Today, Father, I give thanks for your grace, mercy, and love—not only for me but for all who come and follow you. Thank you, sweet Jesus, for choosing me. I get very excited as I sit here in the garden, awaiting to feel your presence and what you will be teaching me on this beautiful sun-filled, hot, muggy morning. Oh, how I love our moments together. As I gaze around at these beautiful surroundings, I watch the trees dance ever so slightly to the warm breeze. It is so peaceful and quiet here. I see you in the distance as you walk towards me. My heart jumps for joy. Your robe is pure white, you wear a beautiful gold belt, and your sandals are brown. Your hair gently blows in the breeze as you walk closer to me. I see your beautiful smile, your teeth as white as the garment you wear. Your eyes sparkle with love. Oh, Father, you are here. Please sit down on the chair next to me. I chuckle as I see the sun in your eyes, and I ask you if you would like shade. Then you bellow out a big laugh and remind me that it's fine, I made the sun. Oh, Jesus, my heart is filled with love and joy as we laugh together. When I was a child, I was raised to believe you were a very serious God. I am so happy to frolic and laugh with you. I am happy to come to know and build a relationship with you. I am so excited to hear what you would like to teach me today. Father, teach me, please.

The Lord answered

"Good morning, my child, I love your heart for me. I love that you are open to my teachings and you are thirsty for more knowledge of me."

"Yesterday, I saw your conversation with a nonbeliever. I saw you become a little disappointed in yourself because you felt you did not have all the answers you thought you needed. I was pleased to see you remember and actually said, 'I sprinkle seeds, that is my job.

My Father will send the harvesters in.' You attempted to make her understand when she said she had never met anyone like you. All you wanted to do was share the peace and love in your heart for me. Now, my child, look out at the beautiful green grass. Do you see that some grass blades are taller than others? The lawn is still beautiful. Some blades just grow faster than others. Meshed together, the lawn is beautiful. You, my child, are like the little grass blade that is still growing. Again, I say that some grow faster than others, that is why, my child, you are not yet a harvester. You are a sprinkler of the seeds of your love for me. Fret not, my child, you have an important job. The grass cannot begin to grow without seeds. Now, go today and wear my name like a banner across your forehead. Jesus, Jesus, Jesus. Trust and believe they will come. I love you, little one. I'm sending you off with blessings today."

And I bless you, sweet Jesus. Thank you for your grace and mercy. Great is thy faithfulness.

*****

For the director of music. Of David, the servant of the Lord. He sang to the Lord the words of this song when the Lord delivered him from the

hand of all his enemies and from the hand of
Saul. He said; I love you Lord, my strength.

—Psalm 18:1

The light shines in the darkness, and
the darkness has not overcome it.

—John 1:5

Teachable Moments

(TEACHING)

Good morning, Father. What a beautiful morning I had with my grandson. He had hurt his shoulder and allowed me to pray for him to heal. He said to me, "Gram, you don't have to pray for everything." I answered, "I know, but thank you for allowing me to pray." He then told me that it doesn't feel better, and I assured him that it would. I then asked him if he would pray with me and to repeat that he accepted you as Lord and Savior. He did. I know he does not understand because he is only hearing the teaching that I give to him. He then said to me, "Gram, look at my sneakers. On the heel it reads, 'Everything is possible if you believe.'" I then told him that they had forgotten to finish the sentence. I explained that it should have read, "Everything is possible for those who believe in Jesus Christ." He is a special child. Thank you again for the beautiful morning. I love that he had those words on his shoes. What a gift from God for him to remember on his feet.

Father, tell me about fear. Why in the Bible does it always say to fear you? My pastor sometimes preaches fear. I choose to respect and reference you as my Father. I know the fruits of the spirit, and you are of love. It bothers me when you are referred to as fear the Lord.

The Lord answered

"Fear not. I am with you [1 John 4:18]. There is no fear in love, but perfect love drives out fear because fear has to do with punishment. The one who fears are not made perfect in love [Isaiah 41:10], so do not fear, I am with you. Do not be dismayed, for I am your God. I will strengthen you and help you. I will uphold you with my righteous right hand. You see, child, the state of love casts out all fear. Stay in the state of love, thinker. A friend said last week that you are a thinker. I gave her that word for you. You are a thinker to a fault. Do not overthink everything. Listen closely to what the Holy Spirit is saying and guiding you to do. Remember, little

one, let go and let God, for I am the truth, the way, and the life. Stop striving for perfection. Remember, I know your heart. I love you, child, now go in peace today with love in heart."

Worry Not, My Child

(TEACHING)

Good morning, Father, I was comfortable sitting by my window, looking out at the garden, when I heard you call to me.

"Come to the garden, child, come, little one, I am waiting here for you. Come to me and rest. I hear your prayers. I see your burdened heart hurting for so many. I see you wanting to teach them of my love and understanding."

Yes, Father, it is true, my heart hurts for those who go off in the wrong direction, wallow in self-pity, or just don't understand your ways. More important, it saddens me that they do not take action. They do not seek to hear your voice, your teachings, your wisdom, as you are the Great Counselor. It takes effort to change, but it does not take great effort to follow you, for you said, "My yoke is easy and my burden is light." Why then, sweet Jesus, do they resist? Or when they come to you to pray, do they do it with their heart and soul? Do they truly believe you are who you say you are, the Son of God, the Most High God?

The Lord Answered

"Little one, be patient with those you encounter. It takes time to come to me, it takes belief. As they say in your world, Rome was not built in a day. Take a look at your own walk. How long has it taken you to come to this place of understanding and learning? It's okay, little one, we all learn in our own time. They will learn. Keep pressing and sprinkling seeds. Be happy, be joyful, and be peaceful. Let them see the beauty and peace and love I provide. Everyone is so preoccupied—work, stress, planning special occasions, running here to there. I loved your saying 'Take time before time takes you.' It is true, child. In their own time, they will learn. Do not judge or find fault with them. Just love them as I love you. It is unconditional and unrelentless love."

"Now look at your garden and see why I asked you to come out. The plants need to be pruned. The tomatoes need to be picked. They grew in their own time.

You did not make them grow, but you nurtured them and watered them—and yes, you even spoke to them. So, now you see I will gently prune those in need. I will tug on their hearts, just as I did to yours. You can see by pruning your plants, it is necessary for them to grow into beautiful and healthy plants. So is my pruning of those who love and come to me. Do not be afraid, my child. I am a gentle loving and forgiving God. I will teach in my loving way. Keep praying for them. Keep love in your heart with forgiveness and thankfulness, and I will make a way. Just as you desire beautiful healthy vibrant plants, I want my children to be fruitful, healthy, and loving. Again, I say, I will make a way. Do not worry about tomorrow, for tomorrow has enough worries of its own. I love you, little one. Go in peace with joy in your heart. Keep your eyes fixed on me, I will show you the way."

"Oh, do not worry about the little tomatoes that fell early and did not grow. My children who follow and love me will grow. Go teach them my sweet child."

Thank you, Jesus, you saw me look at those little tomatoes that fell to the ground. You saw my concern for them. Today, I will walk in love and faith for I believe and love you. I know you are guiding, loving, taking care, and healing those who I bring to you. I am thankful to have been chosen to serve such an awesome God. I am thankful for the price you paid on the cross for us.

I love you, my God, my Lord and Savior. Again, thank you, Jesus.

*****

Therefore I tell you, do not worry about your life, what you will eat or drink; or about your body, what you will wear. Is not life more than food, and the body more than clothes? Look at the birds of the air; they do not sow or reap or store away in barns, and yet your heavenly Father feeds them. Are you not much more valuable than they? Can any one of you by worrying add a single hour to your life? And why do you worry about clothes? See how the flowers of the field grow. They do not labor or spin. Yet I tell you that not even Solomon in all his splendor was dressed like one of these. If that is how God clothes the grass of the field, which is here today and tomorrow is thrown into the fire, will he not much more clothe you—you of little faith? So, do not worry, saying "What shall we eat? Or "What shall we drink?" or "What shall we wear?" For the pagans run after all these things, and your Heavenly Father knows that you need them. But seek first his kingdom and his righteousness, and all these will be given to you as well. Therefore do not worry about tomorrow, for tomorrow will worry about itself. Each day has enough trouble of its own.

—Matthew 6:25-33

Just Call My Name

(TEACHING)

Good morning, Father. You have blessed me with another day. For this, I am most thankful.

I woke up last evening with a severe neck pain. Did I sleep on it in an incomparable position? I asked myself. Nevertheless, I struggle to get out of bed to take something for the pain as well as an ice pack. How do I do this, I ask myself, for I can hardly move, the pain is so great. There was no one to turn to, it was late at night, and who should I call? I turned to you and called your name. "Jesus, Jesus, Jesus, help me," I cried out. And so you did. Slowly, you brought me to my feet. Slowly, you carried me down the stairs to get some ice and pain medication. Thank you, my love, my faithful God. I could not have done it without your help.

As I sit here looking out at the garden this morning, it is soaked from the rain. The air is cool, the day is gray. There is sadness in my heart for all those who suffer not just from physical pain but anxiety, depression, and fear. I know in my heart of hearts, none of this is from you. How do I bring them out of captivity? How do I help them? I ask.

The Lord answered

"Tell them to do what I have instructed you to do in writing 'Cluttered House, Cluttered Mind, Cluttered Body.' Tell them to come to me when they are weary, and I will give them rest. You are learning that in every situation, there is a lesson to be learned. I waste nothing, my child. Tell them not to give in to the pressure in life but to keep their eyes fixed on me. Some lessons are not always easy, but they are necessary for growth."

"Let us look at children, for example. Babies learn to walk. They fall down, they get back up. They fall down and get back up. They soon learn to walk, and now they are running. Why did they continue to get back up? Because their Father was standing near with open arms, saying, 'Come to me, I will catch you. I am your Father, child.' Each trial has a different lesson to be learned. Some are easier than others, and some lessons are very difficult. We all grow at our own pace. I am your

Father. I know what you need to grow strong, vibrant, and healthy to fulfill your destiny here on earth."

"As a baby keeps his eyes fixed on his father and knows without a shadow of a doubt that his father will catch him and keep him from harm, so too am I your father and will always take you from the darkness into the light where I live. Again, I say, come to me when you are weary, come to me when you are hurting. I will refresh you and give you peace. I am your Father, and I love all my children. Come to me with a thankful heart. Learn, child, to take care of your hearts, your minds, and bodies. Nourish them, exercise them, but most of all, give me first place in your heart. Keep your eyes fixed on me, and I will give you the rest."

Thank you, once again, my Great Teacher, wonderful Counselor. I will keep your words close to my heart, and I will go out and teach in your name, the name *Jesus*, who prevails above all names.

*****

Ask and it will be given to you; seek and you will find; knock and the door will be opened to you.

—Matthew 7:7

Do not be anxious about anything, but in every situation, by prayer and petition, with thanksgiving, present your requests to God. And the peace of God, which transcends all understanding, will guard your hearts and your minds in Christ Jesus.

—Philippians 4:6–7

For my yoke is easy and my burden is light.

—Matthew 11:30

Lean On Me

(TEACHING)

Good morning Father, as I sit here on this rainy day looking out at the garden, I am prompted to glance at the tree straight ahead of me. The same tree I see every day but today I notice it leaning to the left. To my surprise, I never noticed it leaning before. Then I heard you whisper "Lean on Me".

Yesterday, at work a very large tree just toppled over and fell into the street for no apparent reason. There was no wind, no rain. I wondered, what would cause this tree to fall?

Sweet Jesus, what message through nature are you speaking to me this morning?

The Lord Answered

"Yes, my sweet little child, I love how you look for my messages. I speak to you through nature.

Lean on Me child, lean on me and you will not fall, it is as simple as that! It pleases me that you are learning to be still, pray and listen to the guidance of the Holy Spirit. The wonderful gift my Father and I have bestowed upon you. Lean on me child, your worries are becoming less and less as you know in your heart of hearts I am guiding you.

You see little one, the tree that fell grew weak, the inside of that tree was hollow, the inside was eaten up and became hollow, too weak to withstand the wind and the rain. It became weak and could not bear the pressure of the environment, and so it fell.

Do not allow this to happen to you! Stay steadfast in my word, stay on your path, worry less. Have faith as tiny as a mustard seed. Think of yourself as that tree when you allow worry, fear, doubt. Into your mind and heart, you become weak, your mind is affected, you get brain fog as it is called in your world. Your body becomes weak with sickness, back pain, headaches to name a few, and some become stricken with disease. Your heart becomes empty and hollow like the inside of the fallen tree. Oh my child this is not from me. I took it all to the cross for you!

I hear you ask, how do I stay strong Father? I will say it again little one, keep your eyes on me. Keep feeding your body proper nourishment, exercise. But, little one keep feeding your mind, your heart and soul with my word as it is written in the Bible. Come to me and I will give you rest.

Now go little one, again I say do not worry about tomorrow, for tomorrow has enough worries of its own. Be like the tree that leans on me. Lean on Me my child, for I will always love you from here to eternity, I will give you rest.

Thank you Jesus, lover of my soul. Your love, grace and mercy is sufficient for me.

*****

I will guide you in the way of wisdom
and lead you along straight paths

Proverbs 4:11

And I will ask the Father and he will give you
another counselor to be with you forever

John 14:16

In the beginning was the word, and the word was God, He was God in the beginning.

John 1:1-2

"Come to me, all you who are weary and burdened, and I will give you rest"

Matthew 11:28.

The Annoying Mosquito

(DISTRACTIONS)

Good morning, Father. I awoke with sadness in my heart for so many hurting people. How blessed am I to be able to sit in my garden with you and not only speak to you but to hear your voice. Once again, I ponder the thought of teaching this beautiful gift to others. It is such a beautiful morning, sweet Jesus, not a cloud in the sky. The birds sing, and the sun provides warmth to my heart and soul. It is amazing how the burdens lift as I once again bring my focus and eyes on you. I begin to be thankful for the beautiful life you have given me and my loved ones. Yes, we too, as your chosen children, must walk through the fire, but the comfort of knowing you are here with me brings light and joy to my heart. Oh, sweet Jesus, thank you again for the Holy Spirit whom I can turn to and call on for guidance. Thank you again for your love and faithfulness.

Oh, this annoying mosquito that buzzes around my head and bites me to cause such itching and discomfort. There it is again, picking at me with a bite here and a bite there. Such a disturbance I will not allow, for my time with you is so very precious and cannot be interrupted. "You cannot live on my blood, mosquito, because my blood is a precious gift from my Savior Jesus. Go away, mosquito, in the name of Jesus." Father, what would you like to say to me about this annoying mosquito?

The Lord answered

"I am the truth, the way and the life. The liar comes to kill, steal, and destroy. Oh, little one, I love how you hear my voice and receive my messages. You are growing. You pulled yourself out of the sadness because you turned to me. Do not fret which church to go to. I am here. I will be wherever you go, for I am with you always. Go where you feel my love and receive my joy. Sing to me, child, with thankfulness in your heart. Your joy is not in a pastor. It is in me, my words, and my spoken words. Go with love and peace in your heart, for wherever you go, I will be there."

"You asked about the mosquito, child. It circles around your head and makes noise. It says, 'I am coming to destroy your peace.' It nips at you and bites you, causing itching and discomfort so you become annoyed and distracted. So too does the liar and the evil one. The spirit of distraction helps to take your eyes off me. My child, it pleases me that you did not allow this distraction to take your eyes off me. You are spiritually stronger than you give yourself credit for. I am well pleased that you understood and are able to overcome what the spirit of distraction attempted to do to take your mind off me. You remained steadfast and recognized the tricks of the enemy. If I be for you, who will be against you? Go in peace today. It does not matter where you worship, just keep me first in your heart as you are now doing. Little one, I want you to lighten up. Have fun, laugh, go with a thankful heart as you praise and worship me. Let it all go, give it to me, and rejoice in my love. Thank you, child, for bringing back your joy that is your gift to me. As you know, little one, my joy is seeing your joy."

Not a cloud in the sky, not a cloud in my heart, not a cloud in my mind. Just you, sweet Jesus, my sunshine!

*****

Jesus answered "I am the way and the
truth and the life. No one comes to
the Father except through me."

—John 14:6

What then, shall we say in response to these
things? If God is for us, who can be against us?

—Romans 8:31

Peace in the Garden

(DISTRACTIONS)

Good morning, Father, another beautiful day is upon us. The only distraction here in the garden is the air conditioner that is loud and noisy. Although it brings comfort to my neighbor, its noise is so distracting to me. Oh Lord, you have heard my cries, and it just turned off. Now I hear the birds singing and the peace and still of the day upon me. Everyone sleeps except the birds, what a beautiful bright sunny morning it is. I pray blessings upon those today that will sing to you, be joyous and save souls for you in the park, for it is an outreach day. Let the rains stay in the heavens, let the sun shine and bring forth the laughter of the children to us. Bring those who you choose come to the park to meet you. Your disciples are waiting with baited breath to scream and shout your name.

They will shout for joy and tell all of your love grace and mercy. They are beautiful disciples with love for you. If they save one soul today, it will be a victory for you. May you bless their work, their voices as they sing and dance for your glory. These are people who serve and love you.

Father, what is your word for me today?

The Lord answered

"Yes, child, the stillness of the morning brings much comfort, peace, and joy. The beauty that surrounds you is a small glimpse of the peace and beauty awaiting you in my kingdom. Do not allow anyone to steal the peace and joy I am providing for you this morning. See the pretty flowers in your flower bed? Do you see the weeds growing close to them, ready to choke them and destroy their beauty? You are my flower, child. Do not allow the weeds of bad thoughts, of disgruntled unhappy people come to infiltrate your beautiful mind and heart for me. Keep them away, little one. It is as simple as keeping your eyes on me. Do not allow the weeds of your thoughts to steal your joy, love, and peace, for this is a gift to you and my followers. Live it, walk with it, and feel agape love

in your heart is all I ask of you. Show them the peace, mercy, and love I have given you. They will come!"

Thank you, sweet Jesus, I will walk in love today for your glory. I will pick those weeds now so they do not choke the beautiful flower of life you have given me. I will release the weeds in my mind so they do not disturb the peace and work you have for me to accomplish.

*****

"Shalom, child, I love you."

*****

But the fruit of the spirit is love, joy, peace, forbearance, kindness, faithfulness, gentleness and self-control. Against such things there is no law.

—Galatians 5:22–23

Faith Reborn

(FAITH BUILDING)

Good morning, Father. Thank you for your love and faithfulness. May I be a vessel you chose, for your grace and sovereign mercy is sufficient for me. The love for you in my heart this morning is overwhelming. Jesus, I recognize the distractions are doing their best to infiltrate my mind and heart, but you have said, "Keep your eyes on me for I am the truth, the way and the life." The other night, I hosted a beautiful prayer and meditation group. I introduced new members who were searching for a place to worship. More importantly, they were hungry for your word. We felt your presence, had a great dinner, and talked of your teachings. After dinner, we gathered around the fireplace and sang songs of worship. The angel fountain gently brought forth the sounds of the gentle flowing water, just as the flow of the living water of life you have given us. As I sat quiet in meditation, a beautiful face of a lion came across my eyes, just his face coming closer to me, so big and beautiful. A lion? I asked. Why did I see a lion? I mentioned my vision to the group, and a member felt it was the Lion of Judah. As you know, I am not well versed in scripture, but I am learning. The desire to know more about this lion quickened me to look for its meaning to find that you are the Lion of Judah and the Lamb of God. Teach me, Father, what would you like to say to me? Why did you show me the face of the lion?

Then I read Revelation 5:5—Jesus was the sacrificial lamb and the Lion of Judah. I also read Genesis 49:8–9: the Lion of Judah is a strong fighter against the enemy.

The Lord answered

"*The lion represents strength, a strong fighter against the enemy. The word enemy upsets you because you do not want to give him the power to know he is lurking around, waiting to stomp on you and attack. You were upset with a pastor's teachings on Sunday when he said you can lose your salvation. You know the truth, child: one who accepts me will never lose their salvation. Worry no more about that, child, keep searching my word. You were also upset that some family members did not understand being born again. You did your best to explain it to them, but you felt inadequate. I give you the lion, a strong fighter against the enemy. The pastor will teach again about spiritual warfare. He is a good teacher and means well, but you do not want to hear it. For now, child, stay focused on my love and peace. Yes, I am the Lion of Judah, as they say. I come to you to remind you of your strength: when you are weak, you become strong. I will strengthen you. I will hold you up with my victorious right hand. Your strength of a lion is me, child. You prayed for a woman in a store, and she showed you her favorite picture: Footprints. One set of footprints, it is I, child, carrying you. Go be the light that shines into the world. I love you."*

And I so love you, Jesus.

Faith as Tiny as a Mustard Seed

(Faith Building)

Wow, Father, it has been six days since we have been here in this intimate moment. I missed you, and yes, I do know you never left my side. But in taking my eyes off you, it has caused me unrest. So many questions I have for you today. I want to be thankful for putting it in my heart to go to Bible study last night. I wanted to stay home and read and study, but you gently encouraged me to go. This is what I have learned, and I am thankful.

Abraham had more faith than a tiny mustard seed to put his son Isaac on the altar and obey your command. What about Isaac obeying his father and not acting like a frightened child but being obedient because his faith in you was unfailing? What a beautiful message. Father, your grace is sufficient for me. Father, I come before you this morning to thank you for your faithfulness and love for me. You know my heart, you know my turmoil. I believe in you, sweet Jesus. Please help me to understand.

The Lord answered

"Change—oh, how you dislike change. You get yourself into a frenzy, yet I know you know that whatever door I have closed, I have opened a better one for you. I know that you know that in your heart of hearts. Stay in the state of peace. You cannot help anyone including yourself if you are in the state of confusion. Do you see it, child? Now accept my gift and believe it. You have learned your lesson well. You were obedient to the Holy Spirit. I know you wanted to stay home and read, but the lesson of faith by Abraham and Isaac was more valuable at this time. Go in peace and love today, for I will always love you."

*****

Then Jesus told him, "Because you have seen me, you have believed; blessed are those who have not seen and yet have believed."

—John 20:29

Now faith is confidence in that we hope for
and assurance about what we do not see. This
is what the ancients were commended for.
By faith we understand that the universe was
formed at God's command, so that what is
seen was not made out of what was visible.

—Hebrews 11:1–3

He replied, "Because you have so little faith.
Truly I tell you, if you have faith as small as a
mustard seed, you can say to this mountain,
'Move from here to there, and it will move.'"

—Matthew 17:20

Just Jump

(FAITH BUILDING)

Good morning, my sweet Father. I am walking, the beautiful sun filled grounds this morning. I am now going to sit here in the garden with you. It has dawned on me that I am far too serious. I look to my right and see you smiling. I hear you say, "You are getting it little one."

The pinwheel in my neighbor's garden goes around and around as it dances to the breeze. You, Father, gently remind me that I am like the pinwheel: I go around and around in circles. My sweet Father, I know you have a lesson to teach me here. Will you please reveal it to me now?

The Lord answered

"I know your desire to love and worship me, my child. I am pleased. You said you give me your heart, you give me your soul, yet you go around and around in circles. Over and over again, you go around and around in this endless circle far too long, little one. It is time for you to jump off the wheel in faith and adhere to my teachings. Listen more attentively to the guidance of the Holy Spirit who dwells within you. For I know the plans I have for you. Jump off, child, jump off and take that leap of faith. I will catch you. I will help and guide you. Again, I say the time is now. Jump off the wheel as on the carousel when you were a child. Take that brass ring that awaits you, for it is from me. You are in for the ride of your life. I will fill you with my agape love, joy, and prosperity so you can go forth and sprinkle seeds of my love to others. Yet again, I remind you that the fruit of the Spirit is love, joy, peace, patience, kindness, goodness, faithfulness, gentleness, and self-control. Against such things, there is no law."

"Take the leap of faith and jump. I chuckle when I hear you tell others, 'I belong to the DIN, DIN club': do it now, do it now. Now practice what you preach, little one, just jump. My loving arms are waiting to catch you *and see you through. You want to glorify me? Join the DIN, DIN club. I love you, little one!"*

Oh, how I love you, Jesus. I am jumping into your loving arms now. You heard my cries, you heard my prayers. Thank you, Lover of my soul. I praise you, I worship you. You are such an awesome God.

*****

Neither height nor depth, nor anything else in all creation, will be able to separate us from the love God that is in Christ Jesus our Lord.

—Romans 8:39

Before they call, I will answer; while they are speaking, I will hear.

—Isaiah 65:24

"For I know the plans I have for you" declares the Lord, "plans to prosper you and not to harm you, plans to give you hope and a future."

—Jeremiah 29:11

A New Direction

(FAITH BUILDING)

Last evening, my friend told me he had a word for me. He saw a wheel and the color green. He said to move forward and release the past. Two weeks ago, another friend also saw a wheel. Now, I saw a wheel with a hamster running on it.

As I sit in prayer and quiet today, I ask you, Lord, what does this wheel mean?

The Lord answered

"You keep going in circles, my love. You cannot move forward because you are going in an endless circle. Jump off the wheel. Go forward for I know the plans for you [Jeremiah 29:11] plans to prosper you and not to

harm you. Give up the past. Behold, I am doing a new thing.

"This is the time for you to move forward, little one. Take care of your health, or more important, put your faith in me and trust and believe you are healed. Stop listening to the outside world. Take your feet out of the cement. You are not stuck. When you saw the video of the man saving a deer from being stuck in the mud, it is an illustration of me pulling you out of the things that break you. Stay out of the past, little one, it is done. Get off the wheel and move forward. Have faith, trust, and believe. My grace is sufficient for you. Go, my child, in peace and love, for this is a new day, a new beginning. Behold, I am doing a new thing."

I love you Jesus.

*****

Forget the former things; do not dwell on the past.

—Isaiah 43:18

Prisoner in My Own Mind

(FAITH BUILDING)

Good morning, Father, thank you for another day. I pray I will use it for your glory and that my light will shine bright with your name—Jesus, Jesus, Jesus—across my forehead, like a banner.

Father, as I reflect on my past journals, I wrote and read that two of my Christian friends saw a wheel. One friend saw the wheel with the color green, and the other friend saw a wheel with a hamster on it. As we sat in the garden together this morning, you showed me a pinwheel and told me for the third time, "Jump off the wheel, I will catch you. Jump, just jump." I heard you say, "You are going around in an endless circle. Go forward, for I know the plans I have for you, plans to prosper you and not to harm you, plans to give you hope and a future, I will bring you back from captivity." Oh, sweet Jesus, I know I am a prisoner in my own mind. What is it that is holding me back? Yet you have been gracious enough to show me a key in a dream. I heard you say it was a key to unlock my fears, my worries, and the doubt in my heart.

Father, I come to you this morning with a humble heart and ask once again, please reveal to me what is it that is holding me back?

The Lord answered

"Your faith, child, it is your lack of faith in yourself. I know your faith in me. I know the time you put into reading my word, hearing my voice, seeking me. Do not doubt yourself, little one, you are worthy of the gifts I am waiting to bestow upon you. I know you will handle my gifts, not hoard them. You will share them. Most of all, I give you the gift of love. I know it is not a physical gift of love that you desire, but it is a gift of love in your heart that you desire to share with others. I said it before, little one, I will say it again: do what you must do to love yourself first. You are deserving of all the beautiful gifts I am waiting to shower you with. Release your mind to me. JUMP, CHILD, JUST JUMP!"

Thank you, sweet Jesus. I release my mind, body, and soul to you and feel your loving arms around me as I jump into them. What better gift could I ask for than to surrender to the King of kings, Lord of lords. I surrender to you, my Love, Lover of my soul.

The Lord answered

"Yes, you did it! You are no longer captive of your own mind. I will be with you, my love, leading and guiding you. My beautiful little one, I know you have made me the lover of your soul, and it brings me great joy. Now go with love in your heart and do not be afraid of the blessings I will bestow on you. You are worthy of my love, you are worthy. I love you, my child, just as you love the children I have given you. Always remember that your love brings me great joy."

*****

I love you, sweet Jesus, the Lover of my soul!

*****

All these blessings will come on you and
accompany you if you obey the Lord your God.

—Deuteronomy 28:2

You will eat the fruit of your labor;
blessings and prosperity will be yours.

—Psalm 128:2

For I know the plans I have for you, declares
the Lord, plans to prosper you and not to harm
you, plans to give you hope and a future.

—Jeremiah 29:11

Rely on the Lord

꧁꧂

(FAITH BUILDING)

Father, you come first. No person, place, or thing comes before you. Good morning, my Jesus. It is a warm cloudy, muggy day. Many would complain, but I choose to see the joy in this day just as the birds do in their singing.

Father, what can I do to glorify you today?

The Lord answered

"Stay in peace with joy and love in your heart. Show the world that to love me means a blessed, joyful, stress-free day because you rely on me, little one, for peace and happiness. I complete you, my child. As you are beginning to recognize, I have given you many blessings: the eyes to see me, the ears to hear me, and the heart

to love. You are doing my work by leading by example. Now, you no longer need to question that I am with you always. In your heart of hearts, show my love, little one, by being happy and peaceful."

"You will see your family prosper. Keep praying, my child, and set up a prayer board. Remember to keep me close and consult with me in every miniscule decision you make. Pray without ceasing till your heart's desire, not only for you and your family, but for all. Those prayers will be met according to my will, my child. I recognize that you put me first today. You will be blessed for your decision. You are learning, little one, and I am pleased."

A Healing Dream

(FAITH BUILDING)

Good morning, Father, my sweet Jesus. I sit here in the garden, awaiting to hear your voice. I reflect on Psalm 42:5: "Why are you downcast, O my soul? Why so disturbed within me? Put your hope in God for I will yet praise him my Savior and my God."

Many emotions are going through me this morning. The children starting new lives in college brings me joy that you have blessed them with these beautiful gifts. You, Jesus, have provided them with a great opportunity to give back to the world and help many people. For these wonderful gifts, I am thankful. However, Father, I am also sad for the children who are hurting and struck with sickness. My heart hurts for all of their parents and loved ones who are carrying this burden with them. What can I do besides pray for them with a thankful heart that they are healed in your name, the mighty name of Jesus?

Father, last evening, you blessed me with a dream. I recall a man talking to people. I believe he was healing them. I was speaking to this man, and he disappeared. I saw him sitting, and he disappeared. I kept saying, "Where is he, where did he go?" Then a banner with your name came across my eyes. "Jesus," it read. I was saying, "I am healed." Things were coming up before my eyes. One appeared like a white tube. These things were coming up and leaving. I woke up and heard myself saying, "I am healed, I am healed."

I began to watch a healer on a video. He said all who were watching would be healed. Thank you, sweet Jesus. I believe it was confirmation that you had already healed me. I have the power of you, Jesus, within me. There is power in your name, Jesus. Yesterday, I was listening to the song "Break Every Chain." I began to think I should write about that. I heard it sung, "There is power, power, power in the name Jesus." Thank you, Jesus. You are so faithful. You have taken our sins to the cross. You have taken our healing and troubles to the cross. What an awesome God we serve! I have the mighty name of Jesus.

I have the Holy Spirit who dwells within me. What more do I need!

The Lord answered

"All you need is trust, faith, and belief in me. You are getting stronger, little one. Rest in me. Remain steadfast in my word. Do not falter now, you are so close. Go with a thankful heart and only speak words of healing and thankfulness for not only yourself but those hurting sick children and for all you encounter. Everyone has different crosses that they carry. Pray with a thankful heart that they come to know my love, my grace, and my mercy. Trust and believe, that is all I ask. It is indeed a hot morning here in the garden. Enjoy the peace and the healing it provides. Remember to be joyful as your joy brings me much joy!"

Thank you for my healing and the healing of these children I bring to you, the children that are in your care. Thank you, my Lord and Savior, for joining me in this hot, peaceful garden filled with your peace, love, mercy, and grace.

Shalom, my Father.

*****

You keep in perfect peace those whose minds
are steadfast, because they trust in you.

—Isaiah 26:3

With trumpets and the blast of the ram's horn—
shout for joy before the Lord, the King.

—Psalm 98:6

Shouts of a joy and victory resound in
the tents of the righteous; "The Lord's
right hand has done mighty things!

—Psalm 118:15

The Sun Shines through the Clouds

(INSPIRATION)

Good morning, my sweet and gentle Father. As I look out the glass door through the raindrops into the garden, a feeling of sadness comes over me. Father, why do I feel sad this morning?

The Lord answered

"Look beyond the raindrops, my child, look to the heavens. The clouds will pass, and the sun will shine bright, just as the clouds will pass in your heart. Oh, my child, when sadness comes, it is because you have taken your eyes off me. Once again, I remind you that things will come up in your life as you walk with me. The left

hand, little one, put all the things the evil one tries to destroy your peace with and give them to me. Now take your left hand that signifies lack of peace and put them in your right hand. I will help you, I will lead you, I will always love you. Focus, child, stay in my word, for I am the truth, the way, and the life. You will go in peace today and feel my joy. As you know, your joy gives me such joy. Now look over at the garden, child. I have given you sunshine for a very brief moment. I am here, little one, I am here. I have never left your side. I know your struggles, but I also know your strength to overcome them. Now take my love and pass it on to someone today, for I will always love you."

Thank you, sweet Jesus, yes, I saw the sun. It peeked out for only a brief second. I knew it was a gift from you as you heard my cries. Oh, how blessed I am to have you in my life, my heart, and my soul. You are the lover of my soul. It is dark again and the rain comes down hard, but the sun shines bright in my heart. It is your light that will never leave me as long as I keep my eyes on you. I praise you. I worship you and will walk with a thankful heart for your glory. Oh, how I love you, sweet Jesus!

"And I am blessed that you chose to follow me. Now go help my people. Now go today with a thankful heart."

*****

Yet I am always with you; you hold me by my right hand. You guide me with your counsel, and afterward you will take me into glory.

—Psalm 73:23–24

Looking Forward

(INSPIRATION)

Lord, what does it mean when you showed me Genesis 19:26? "But Lot's wife looked back and she became a pillar of salt."

The Lord answered

"Don't look back, little one. The past is done. Take what you have learned from me and be thankful. People come into your life only for a season. I placed them there to teach you what I need you to learn. Don't look back. There are many blessings ahead for you and your family. You get stuck because you take your eyes off me. Stop trying so hard. Where is that beautiful little girl I met in the convent? Focus on that day of peace and tranquility. There was no one there to make fun of how slow you

worked or how your heart searched for me. I accepted you totally then, and I accept you now with your faults and transgressions. You see, I know your heart and soul. I know you aim to love and please me. I know you want others to know me as you do, but this takes time. Do not feel bad. Don't allow anyone to place guilt on you, for my love is not of guilt and fear. My love is perfect in all ways. I have blessed you, my child, do you see it? Do you see the time I have given you to spend with me? Do not squander it in self-pity or loneliness, for I am with you always. I have given you a thirst of knowledge of me. Remember Harry's words 'He is your best Lover, let him lead the way.' It is I who told him to send that to you. Stay on the path I am leading you, and you and your family will be rewarded. Give your concerns to me. I will see that your family is safe. You see the growth in them, now I ask you, little one, to see the growth in yourself. Stop being so hard on yourself. Spread love and joy. Reflect on my son, Jesus. He did not walk in fear, sorrow, self-pity, or procrastination. I have made you in his image. His ways are my ways—they will be your ways. I see your mind start to wander. Come back to me little one. Keep your eyes on Jesus, for he is the truth, the way, and the life. Now go in peace and enjoy this day I have given you. Exercise, pay your bills, and get ready, for I have much work for you to do. I love you, little one."

And I love you, thank you, Father.

God's Presence

(INSPIRATION)

Good morning, my Father. As I invite you onto my bench this morning, the sun is shining so bright, and I feel the warmth of it on my body. A slight breeze is ever so comfortable. The birds are singing joyfully for us. Oh, how I wish I could understand what they are singing, but you can, Father. You sit on the chair on the right side of me. I have been blessed to watch you walk to me by the wonderful path of greenery and trees. As I invite you to sit next to me, I chuckle because I asked if the sun in your eyes is too uncomfortable for you. We both chuckle then when you replied, "I am God, I can shade the sun if I want to, after all, little one, I made it." Your eyes are beautiful. They are green, and your hair is long and sandy-brown colored. You are wearing a white robe and brown sandals. Oh, how I wish I could touch you, but I can place my heart in your hands and feel your peace just as I did as a child when we first met in the convent. What is so funny is that I used to go there and ask to clean and dust the chapel. My mother never understood this because I disliked cleaning. I would work in slow motion, in peace and love. Your presence was strong, and though I was a child, I could feel and know you were there. Just as I know you are here with me now. Thank you, Jesus. I praise you and honor you. I felt the healing of what I thought was a heart attack during a worship service. My chest was gripped in pain, but as I sang your praises and thanked you, the pain lifted, and peace came over me. I felt you pass by me in the form of a slight breeze. I opened my eyes and looked up to see if there were any air-conditioning vents over me, but there weren't any. My friend who was standing next to me was gone. I then knew it was you, sweet Jesus, healing me. Oh, how you have taken care of me! Oh, how many times I can see your hand helping and healing and caring for me.

Father, I come to you this morning with total thankfulness in my heart. You know my heart, and I now know you are a God of mercy and kindness.

The Lord answered

"Keep your eyes on me. Teach your family and all the lives you touch to keep their eyes on Jesus, for I am the truth, the way, and the life. Do not be deceived by the false voices of Satan. Keep your eyes, ears, and heart on me. I am your God, I am your savior, I am your best lover, let me lead the way. Now go in peace, dear little one, with joy and thankfulness in your heart. Know that I am taking care of you and your family. I have given you many blessings. Keep speaking to your family and lead by example. Peace be with you, my child. Pray for all you said you would lift up in prayer. My blessings are with you and your family today. Actually, if you remember, I have entrusted you to take care of my children as well. You are doing well. Keep going, little one. I enjoy the morning chats we have, and I am with you always."

I smile as I watch him smile back at me. He will never leave me and all who have their eyes to see and their ears to hear him.

Thank you Jesus!

Opened Eyes

(INSPIRATION)

Good morning, Father. Thank you for this day. Thank you for opening my eyes and ears to hear your voice. As I sit in the quietness and stillness this morning, I hear you say once again, "Do not go before me, wait upon the Lord." And so I shall.

Fill my heart with love and peace today so I may show my family and others that I live this way because you, Jesus, have placed this ever so gently on my heart. I am to be thankful to be learning more about the angels through my studies. The only attention I shall seek, Father, is from you. Let me lead by example with you by my side.

Thank you for keeping my family and friends safe today. Help me to give others a word of encouragement if they should come to me. I want to make sure that my motives are correct and from you. I await your answer in prayer with a discerning heart.

I love you, Jesus, thank you.

Focus on Me

(INSPIRATION)

Father, it has been days since I actually quieted myself down to hear your voice. Speak to my heart, please.

The Lord answered

"Oh, my child, yes, I have endured much pain on the cross for all my children. Focus on my resurrection. Focus on the joy that together we will live in everlasting peace. Focus on my victory. Focus on your victory to come. I know your heart, I know you are saddened by the pain I endured. But I want you to focus on the victory. Rejoice and be glad. The enemy has come to steal that joy. I have come to give you joy. Be happy, my child. Do not focus on what is going on in the world. Do not be

afraid. Fear is not from me. Go in peace today. Listen to your Holy Spirit. Feel the love and joy in your heart. The beauty you demonstrated last night came from the inner glow from me. You have too many distractions again this morning. Come to me when you are in a quiet mode with no interruptions. I love you, my child."

Rest in Me

(INSPIRATION)

Lord, I draw near with a sincere heart, washed by the blood of my Lord and Savior, Jesus Christ. I set aside my reasoning, my thoughts, my theology, my fears, and my pride. I relax, cease my striving, and tune in to your flow within. Holy Spirit, I open my heart and mind to you. I ask that you anoint the eyes of my heart and enlighten my understanding. I ask that you grant me God's thoughts, God's pictures, God's emotions, and God's creativity. Thank you for what you reveal in Jesus's name. Amen.

Father, what is next for me?

The Lord answered

"Rest, my child, rest in me. I will show you the way. Put your mind to sleep and go enjoy today. Perhaps a memory will be jarred when you see the nuns. Be thankful for this day. Your answers will come. Listen to the Holy Spirit's guidance. Learn more to rely on him. Keep walking, keep on your path. I will show you the way. I will direct your steps. You want immediate answers. You must trust and believe. Walk in faith, not by sight. You will see and feel what is right. I will direct your path through the Holy Spirit. Walk with joy and peace in your heart. Lead by example."

"I love, you, child and remember I know your heart so therefore I say again, 'Do not be anxious about anything, but in every situation, by prayer and petition, with thanksgiving, present your requests to God. And the peace of God, which transcends all understanding, will guard your hearts and your minds in Christ Jesus.'"

Changing Seasons

(Inspiration)

I sit here this morning gazing out my window, the sky is gray, the seagulls flying high, and there is a blanket of new fallen snow. It is so pure and clean and perfectly untouched, just as Jesus brought us into this world. In a few days, the snow will be trampled on and dirty and give no joy. It reminds me of what we humans do to ourselves. We burden ourselves with worry, fear, sorrow, procrastination, self-pity to say the least, and we become tainted. Did you ever notice the faces of unhappy people? How distorted they look from anger or depression and sadness? I feel so sad for them.

I am looking at the beautiful birds. They do not have a care in the world. They do not worry about food or clothing. Jesus said, "If I take care of the birds, surely, I will take care of you, for you are more valuable." As I reflect on this cold long winter season, awaiting spring, it reminds me of the seasons in life that we must go through. We are going through another season of change as I take care of health issues. It is all good.

So, today, I will continue on my journey and be thankful for my blessings. I wait upon the Lord to show me the way. I am so thankful for having him in my life. Today, I will enjoy this precious present.

What Now?

(INSPIRATION)

Father, what now?

The Lord answered

"I say it again, my child, trust and believe. Keep your eyes on me. Relax in me. Go exercise and heal. Be joyful in peace and decisions made. I am doing work through you. Do not worry about tomorrow, for tomorrow has enough worries of its own. Stay focused on me. I will guide you and show you the way."

"Your success will glorify me because you will be able to bring more people to me. Unclutter your mind, child, I see the wheels turning. It is not you. It is I who guides you. How can you hear my voice if your mind is full of worry? I told you I will lead the way. Follow me *with love and peace in your heart, and I will guide you. I love you, child. When you pray for someone, seek my face first. Ask me how to minister them. Picture me there next to you. Open your mouth, and I will fill it. Rely on my words, not yours. Do not worry about making a mistake. Trust and believe in me, for my love and guidance is perfect. Let my will be done, not yours."*

*****

I am the Lord your God, who brought
you up out of Egypt. Open wide
your mouth and I will fill it.

—Psalm 8:10

Between a Rock and a Hard Place

(INSPIRATION)

Good morning, my Love, my dear Father. As I look out the window at the wet, soaked garden from the fierce storm that came by last evening, I see a leaf. It appears to get caught up on a web. It dangles in the air. It floats to whichever the way the breeze takes it. It is stuck in what I will call limbo, unable to move from one position to another. Stuck between a rock and a hard place, shall we say.

How does one move from a hard place to a rock? You, sweet Jesus, are the rock. I see discouragement. I see exhaustion. I see anxiety as to where to turn. I see frustration. It is heartbreaking to watch. I suggest seeking God first for our answers. I have, is the reply, he does not answer me. How then, Father, do I advise them? How do I make them understand you are here with them, your timing is perfect, and your plan for their lives is perfect? I know you took all their pain to the cross. They follow you, they know you, they love you, they seek to hear your direction. What then, sweet Jesus, do I say to them?

The Lord answered

"I see them, child. I see their struggles. I see and hear them, their prayers. Tell them as I have told you, 'Rest and know that I am God.' I will make a way—this is my promise to all who love and believe in me. Teach them to rest in me. I am doing work in them; I am teaching them to remain steadfast in my word. I will keep them safe. I am watching over them. Tell them to keep their words and thoughts positive. I will send a helper. I will make a way, for I know the plans I have for them. Plans to prosper them and keep them well. I have given my children tremendous strength. They are fighters. They do not give up, I see that. They are growing weary, but together, they are growing strong. Their combined strength will see them through. They can't hear my direction because their minds are full of static from worry. Tell them to rest in me. Take time and rest their weary minds, hearts, and souls in me. Once again, I say, 'Be still and know I am God, I will make a way.'

"*Now you go and release the leaf that is stuck in limbo. Let it reach its destiny. Tell the children to release it all to me so that I can take them to their destiny. I can, and I will fulfill my promise to take care of them, prosper them, keep their health strong, and guide them. I will show them the way, but they must give their cares and worries to me. I am the Great Counselor. I will make a way. Now, go with peace and love in your heart and do not stop praying. I've got this! My love will prevail for my children. My grace and mercy will prevail for them.*"

It is done! The leaf gave me a little resistance. It did not want to let go, but it now reached its destiny with all the other leaves, so too are we stubborn and find it difficult to let go. What a wonderful lesson. Let go and let you, God, do your work in us for your grace, mercy, and love endure forever. Thank you for taking care of my family and all those who come to you with a humble heart. I trust and believe in you, sweet Jesus, for I know your word does not return void.

*****

"For I know the plans I have for you," declares
the Lord," plans to prosper you and not to harm
you, plans to give you hope and a future."

—Jeremiah 29:11

For we live by faith, not by sight.

—2 Corinthians 5:7

I can do all this through him who
gives me strength.

—Philippians 4:13

Dream of a Flowered Box

(INSPIRATION)

Good morning, Jesus. Last evening at 1:06 a.m., I had a dream of a flowered box. It was a picture that came across my eyes of this flowered box. I was awakened, and I heard you say, "Go find the flowered box." I stumbled out of bed in a stupor. I remembered going through my closet and all my dresser drawers. I could not find this flowered box. I didn't even recall ever seeing a flowered box. I spoke out to you and said, "Lord, I cannot find the flowered box, and I am tired. I will look for it in the morning." Then my spirit heard you say, "Go look in your closet in the sewing box." But I had already looked in the closet and the sewing box was covered with other boxes.

"Really?" I asked, so on my hands and knees, I removed the other boxes, and there was the sewing box. I opened it and was surprised at what I found.

There it was, the flowered box I saw in my dream. As I opened the box, something fell out. I looked down at my arm, and I saw a crochet holder with a cross on it. To my surprise, there was a note that read,

I carry a cross in my pocket. A simple reminder to me of the fact that I am a Christian no matter where I may be.

This little cross isn't magic, nor is it a good luck charm.

It isn't meant to protect me from physical harm.

It's not for identification for all the world to see.

It's simply an understanding between the Savior and me.

When I put my hand in my pocket to bring out a coin or a key, the cross is there to remind me of the price he paid for me.

It's also a daily reminder of the peace and comfort I share with all who knows my master and give themselves to his care.

So I carry a cross in my pocket, reminding no one but me that Jesus Christ is Lord of my life, if only I'll let him be.

As I continued to take out the items one by one, I asked, "Father, what does all this mean?"

The Lord answered

"The stretch hair band—I am stretching you child."

"The nail—it is a reminder of the pain and all I have endured and taken to the cross for you."

"The paper clip—a reminder that it is I, child, that is holding you together."

"A medal of St. Jude, the patron saint of the impossible—a reminder that nothing is impossible for those who believe."

"A pretty blue flower—I bring you peace, child."

"A beautiful butterfly pin—you are in a metamorphosis for me," I heard him say.

Father, I am so thankful for your love and faithfulness. My family and I will stand firm in your love, grace, and mercy. We will keep our eyes on you, Jesus, the Lord and Savior of our life.

The Lord answered

"Oh, my child, your heart and eyes are opened to receive my love and messages. Stay steadfast. Keep your eyes on me. Teach your family to keep their eyes on me. Do not look at the world. Help others to know my love.

The sound of the demons you hear are a reminder of the enemy trying to tear you down. Do not listen to the noise, and be thankful in your transgressions that you are able to bring them to me. Keep listening and stay close to the one who dwells in you. I have given you the Holy Spirit. Abide in me. Get going on your assignment to show how to hear my voice. Be thankful for the family I have entrusted to you to protect and lead. Go, little one, with joy and thankfulness in your heart. Pray for the world, pray for peace, and say my name, Jesus. Spread love, not fear. There is no fear in my perfect love. Grow from what I am showing you. I love you, child."

Thank you, Jesus, and I will always love you.

A Bird's-Eye View

(INSPIRATION)

Good morning, Father. I invite you into my writing and my heart today. I see you sitting on my deck. You have brought with you a pigeon that sits very still and quiet on top of the chair pillow. You remind me to wait upon the Lord.

The Lord answered

"See the bird. He does not worry, he does not have a care in the world. He does not worry where his food comes from or how high he can fly, or if he will be attacked by the raven. He knows I am taking care of him."

"So, my children, my sweet little one, if I will take care of the birds, will I not take care of you? For you *surely are more valuable than the birds. Go in peace today, little one, with joy in your heart. Cast all of your cares and burdens on me, for my grace is sufficient for you."*

"Walk in faith, not by sight. I love you little one."
Thank you, Jesus, I love you too.

*****

Therefore I tell you, do not worry about your life, what you will eat or drink; or about your body, what you will wear. Is not life more than food, and the body more than clothes? Look at the birds of the air; they do not sow or reap or store away in barns, yet your Heavenly Father feeds them. Are you not much more valuable than they? Can any one of you by worrying add a single hour to your life?

—Matthew 6:25–34

Jesus Is My Rock

(FEAR)

Good morning, Father. I came to the garden to wait for you. As always, you were here before me, for you never leave my side. Thank you for your watchful eye and healing over my family.

Father, yesterday, I was challenged by fear. I took the sword of your word and slayed that dragon. I admit it was a battle, but you, my Father, the Lover of my soul, were there for me and with me. You held me up with your victorious right hand. I asked a follower of yours to pray for me and a family member in need of surgery. In his cool, calm, collected, way he said "Sure." As I sat next to him listening to our pastor's teachings on healing, he turned to me and said, "God said you know what to do."

"I know what to do?" I asked. I became frantic and replied, "I will take out my sword, I will cut down the enemy, and I will cast out demons. I will take out my sword, the word of God as it is written in scripture and do battle." Then a feeling of peace and quiet came upon me, and I heard your sweet whisper in my ear. "Be still and know that I am God." I smiled, chuckled to myself as I rested in your presence. Thank you for the Holy Spirit who dwells within me.

Father, how did you see me in this encounter? Will you give me a word I can take to your people who have the same struggles, fears, and doubts?

The Lord answered

"Good morning, my daughter. I have sent you a mourning dove that you still hear cooing. Take the peace and beauty and enjoy it. Fear is still trying to grip you. I am pleased that you recognized it and came to me. Yes, child, let the Lion of Judah roar so loud that you cannot hear what fear is saying. I gave you the vision of the lion when you were in prayer and meditation. When you were a child, you were such a frightened little girl. You were afraid of so many things, but your childhood is gone. You are growing up in me. I saw your struggles yesterday, but I also saw your determination and strength

to keep your eyes on me, child. I am pleased with you, little one, why are you not pleased with yourself? I will say it again, little one, as I have said before: stay on your path. You will conquer fear and doubt today and be thankful for the healing I am providing for your family."

Thank you, Jesus, I am tired of this same battle. When will I conquer it? When will I feel your perfect agape love, as there is no fear in your perfect love?

The Lord answered

"You are so close, little one. Now take the rock and smash it. Pick up pebbles of joy, love, peace, and healing, as they are yours, child. You already possess them. Cherish them and bring them forth to others. Teach by being a living example. Implement the strategy I have given you. Do not tire, do not hunger, do not fear, and do not worry, for I am with you always."

*****

I will stand there before you by the rock at
Horeb. Strike the rock, and water will come
out of it for the people to drink." So, Moses
did this in the sight of the elders of Israel.

—Exodus 17:6

Rejoice in the Lord always. I will
say it again: Rejoice!

—Philippians 4:4

Respect vs. Fear

(FEAR)

Lord, why must I keep reading that you should be feared? I choose to see you as a God and Heavenly Father of love.

The Lord answered

"Oh, my child, I commend you for not wanting to fear me. You truly understand who I am. Fear has many interpretations. People understand fear, but you understand the respect, love, and commandments I desire. I do not want to hurt you—that is not my desire. I do want you to know there are consequences to sin as you have found out. You have learned I have shed my blood and covered you. If I have done this for you and forgiven you and you believe my word, why *have you not forgiven yourself? You have seen the torment that some have gone through—that is not what I want for my children. I allow these things to be seen by you so that you can teach others. Would you give a small child a hot cup of coffee or a knife to play with? No, of course not, but as he got older, they would learn to respect these and use them properly. That is all I want from you. Obedience is not always easy. Like a little colony of ants, you go off out of line, but it is I who brings you back. You have challenges ahead of you, my child. Remember Jeremiah 29:11: for I know the plans I have to prosper you and not to harm you. I brought you through that, did I not?"*

"So, my dear little one, I need you to strengthen your body, get physically fit. Feed your body the proper nourishment. Feed your heart and soul with my word. I delight in you. I want you to delight in me. My grace is perfect for you and your family. Keep going in the right direction. You will be able to help many people once you understand them and back them up with scripture."

I will, Lord. Thank you for putting that desire in my heart. I will be a helper to many in the name of Jesus, to be used to glorify you and save souls. I love you, Jesus. I place my family in your hands.

Feelings

(FEAR)

Help me to decipher my feelings, Father.

The Lord answered

"Be still and know that I am God."

"You are still trying to rush before me. I have given you the gift of time, yet you squander it in self-pity and loneliness. Why do you not feel joyful in the rest I have given you? Why must you be so analytical of everything? You ruminate over and over again. Did I not tell you I was taking care of your family? Do you not believe me, or do you think you can do a better job yourself? Stop trying to control every situation and circumstance. Stop looking at what others are doing. They are of the world, and you are not. You are mine. Guilt is not from me.

I have given you a discerning heart and spirit. Don't just walk away from unfinished business. Keep your eyes on me, little one, for I am the truth, the way, and the life. Come to me. I told you I have much for you to do. Get out of yourself and more involved in my work. Remember, my child, fear is not of me. I am peace, love, and mercy. I will say it again: do not take your eyes off me. Lighten up and go have some fun today. I have my hand on you. Plant seeds so I may gain more souls. I have you, my child, de-stress."

*****

So do not fear, for I am with you; do not be dismayed for I am your God. I will strengthen you and help you with my righteous right hand.

—Isaiah 41:10

A Missed Opportunity

(COMPASSION)

Good morning, Father, the rain fall heavy in the garden. The wind blows, the trees sway, and even the birds are quiet. A glimpse of the sun attempts to peek out, and I have perceived it to say, "I am here, child, I am with you."

Father, yesterday, I had an opportunity to help a hurting woman to sell her costume jewelry. She needed money to help her daughter travel home. I repent for my sin of lack of compassion for her. I became irritated as it was closing time and I wanted to go home. I did not acknowledge her pain, even when she told me she had no colon. She was so thin and frail. I turned her over to another associate because I did not want to work with her. Jesus, you would never have done that. I say I want to walk the earth as you did, but clearly, I did not. I could have taken money from my wallet to give to her, but I did not. I repent for my sin of lack of compassion. I repent for my sin of disappointing others, but most off all, you. I missed opportunity to share your love and pray for her. Sweet Jesus, why did I react this way? Were you as disappointed in me as I was of myself?

The Lord answered

"Look at the raindrops on the glass door. See two of the drops falling? These are my tears for you, little one. I see your pain. I know your heart. It is true you were consumed with yourself, your own desire to leave and go home. You are human, child. You recognize your sin of lack of compassion and repented for your sin. I see that, and it pleases me. You are much too hard on yourself. You cannot give money to everyone that comes in to sell their wares. Many are using the money for drugs. Discernment—I will give you discernment for future encounters. Pray for her now, little one. It is never too late to pray for those in need. Stay steadfast in my word, little one, for when you are weak, you are strong. Strengthen yourself physically, mentally, and spiritually. I did not put you in these situations to be perfect. I put you here to learn. So you made a mistake. I have forgiven you, now go forth with love in your heart and lead by example.

Now, little one, I have forgiven you, now forgive yourself. Pick yourself up, dust yourself off, and start all over again, for I have more lessons for you to learn."

Thank you, Jesus, there is a valuable lesson in all we encounter. Thank you for being the loving, caring, and teaching God that you are. Thank you for the pain you endured on the cross for us. I will go forward today with love in my heart and remember that "if God be for me, who can be against me?" Thank you for the lesson. I love you, sweet Jesus.

*****

That is why, for Christ's sake, I delight in weakness, in insults, in hardships, in persecutions, in difficulties. For when I am weak, then I am strong.

—2 Corinthians 12:10

For we are live by faith, not by sight.

—2 Corinthians 5:7

Thankful Thoughts

(BLESSINGS)

Good morning, sweet Jesus. Today, fear and doubt came upon me like a thief in the night. Forgive me, my Father, I have taken my eyes off you and consumed my heart with worry. You have told me over and over again to not worry about your family. "I'm taking care of them," you have said to me. Forgive me for my unfaithfulness and doubt. Sweet Jesus, your grace is sufficient for me. Today, I will be thankful for all the wonderful gifts you have given me. Today I will keep my eyes on you and see the beauty in everything and everywhere.

I am thankful for your words "Have faith as tiny as a mustard seed. Go and you can move a mountain."

Today, I am thankful for my family and their accomplishments.

Today, I am thankful for my friends that follow you.

Today, I am thankful to have the eyes to see, the ears to hear, and the voice to speak.

Today, I have thankfulness in my heart for my health.

Today, I am thankful for my finances.

Today, I am thankful I can sit on my deck and hear the birds sing,

Today, I am thankful you are with me always.

Today, I am thankful for you, Father God, who has given your son who took so much punishment to save my soul.

Today, I am thankful for the Holy Spirit who dwells inside me.

Today, I am thankful to be able to strengthen my body.

Today, I am thankful I will finally take control once and for all and heal myself with your guidance and grace.

Today I am thankful for the people you send me to mentor.

Most of all, Father, I am thankful I have you in my life.

Thank you, Jesus

By Faith, Not Sight

(BLESSINGS)

Oh, my Father, this morning, I just want to tell you that I love you and I am thankful to you for the wisdom and peace you have imparted on me. I will not go by sight but will go with trust and belief that you are doing work in me and my family.

I thank you for the time we have spent this morning and the work you are giving me for your glory.

I will go in peace, Father. Your grace is sufficient for me.

I love you, Jesus.

*****

My yoke is easy and my burden is light.

—Matthew 11:30

A Proclamation of Faith

(BLESSINGS)

I want to thank you, Father for a wonderful birthday yesterday. I have been blessed by you with the most amazing family and so many friends and acquaintances. Thank you for your love and faithfulness and what you have done by giving up your life for us. Father, your grace is sufficient for me.

Father, I am trying to be still so I can hear your voice. Forgive my lack of faith that I still cloud my mind with worry. I rebuke all the voices in my mind that want to hold me from you and the blessings you have waiting for all of us. You, sweet Jesus, are my Lord and Savior and will restore peace, love, wisdom, and prosperity to my family. You, Father, are the truth, the way, and the life. I thank you, Father God, for giving us your only son. Jesus, you have suffered and died for us so that we may live in eternal glory with you and your Father. I am thankful for the Holy Spirit who dwells in my heart and soul and guides me according to your will, not mine. Oh, my Lord and Savior, I love you so.

I proclaim victory in love, peace, wisdom, health, and prosperity for my family. I proclaim safety to all I know. I proclaim blessings to all as well.

You are a God of mercy, kindness, and love. You said you will "light the lamp beneath my feet and lead the way."

Today and every day, Father, I choose to follow you. I pray to save as many souls as I can for you, my Father, so that when we join you in heaven, we can all celebrate your goodness, kindness, and love, in the name of Jesus.

*****

Your word is a lamp for my feet,
a light on my path.

—Psalm 119:105

From Here to Eternity

(BLESSINGS)

Good morning, Father. The calm after the storm is so quiet and peaceful. Last evening, the roar of the thunder was so loud, the lightning was fierce. Someone posted a picture of the lightning bolts. Both my daughter and I saw a beautiful very large angel in between the bolts of lightning. Father, you have given us the eyes to see, and we are so thankful. Now, this morning, there is total peace in the garden. The trees are still, the birds are still, the serenity is amazing. Thank you for this gift. As I await to feel your presence and hear your voice, I am thankful for everything you have blessed me with. I asked you for a bright sunny apartment to live in, but you gave me so much more. You gave me a beautiful bright and sunny home. You gave me a beautiful garden to meet with you, to sit and pray with you. I am so thankful for your Faithfulness and love, my Lord.

Father, again, you have given me so much, and for that, I am in awe of your grace and mercy. I am indeed so thankful. Today, I ask for wisdom to help those in need of understanding so that they may open their eyes to see and feel your love, grace, and mercy.

The Lord answered

"Oh, my child, do you see what appears to be a spiderweb just floating in the air with two little white eggs attached to it? I see you looking closely at it. What is it you ask, where does it end, where does it begin? Well, look closely child. You can see it begins on the chair, but it just appears to be floating in the air. You cannot find or see the end. It floats in the air with no end in sight. So too is my grace, mercy, and love for you and all those who choose to follow, worship, and love me. My love for you endures forever. There is no end, sweet little one. When it is time, I will take you to eternity where my love endures forever."

"For today, my child, enjoy the present. Go to the beach as planned and enjoy the wonders of the earth. As I told you before, it is only a glimpse of what is yet to

come for my loved ones. Go today and bask in love and the precious present. Listen closely to the Holy Spirit. Do not go before him. I love you, my sweet little one."

"The spider appeared and ran across your arm. You are okay, little one, you are safe."

*****

As always, I love you, sweet Jesus, Lover of my soul. Thank you.

Epilogue

T hank you, Jesus, the power of your love is nothing to be reckoned with. Truly, you are the son of God. Truly, you gave your life for us. Truly, you are our beloved Father. Your grace is sufficient for us. I pray with a thankful heart, for your obedience to our father in accepting the daunting and painful task of taking and nailing our sins to the cross.

Father, as I bring this book to a close, what message would you like me to bring to your followers?

The Lord answered

"Tell them as I have told you, I WANT TO BE YOUR EVERYTHING! I want all my love I give to you to be received with thanksgiving in your heart. I want you to have an open mind and heart to receive all the blessings I am waiting to bestow on you. Yes, I want to be your everything. I want to be your father, the lover

of your soul, your provider, your El Shaddai, your counselor, your comforter, your healer, your strength, your kindness, your peacemaker. I say it again, I WANT TO BE YOUR EVERYTHING!

I love all my children. Tell them to go in peace and know their father loves them. Stay close to me. Listen more closely to the guidance of the Holy Spirit. Learn to recognize his voice and love for you. Seek my word and blessings will flow unto them.

Now go child, with love and peace in your heart. Know, trust and believe you are the children of the most high God. You are the sons and daughters of the King of kings. Now walk in peace and love today. I am right here by your side."

Thank you, Jesus. I hope all who read this book will receive your words. I love you Jesus, lover of my soul. I pray this book is a comfort and blessing to all who read it.

*****

"For I know the plans I have for you", declares the Lord, "plans to prosper you and not harm you, plans to give you hope and a future. Then you will call upon me and come and pray to

me and I will listen to you. You will seek me
and find me when you seek me with all your
heart. I will be found by you" declares the Lord,
"and I will bring you back from captivity."

—Jeremiah 29:11-14

Notes

Notes

Notes

Notes

About the Author

MaryLou DeCarlo lives on Long Island with her family, friends, and faith. She never set out to be an author. Her main goal was to strengthen her relationship with God. She found her most peaceful place was either in her garden or, when weather didn't permit, looking out to it. As she began to meditate and read her Bible, she began to hear God's voice and realized how, by journaling, she was being taught valuable lessons. She was advised in her sessions with Jesus that she should "sprinkle seeds" to others. That was the role he had gifted to her. He also told her to share his counseling with others by putting many of his lessons in this book.

Please visit MaryLou on her website at: MaryLouDeCarlo.com